GEMSTONES,
CRYSTALS AND HEALING

Thelma Isaacs, PhD

Lorien House
P.O. Box 1112
BLACK MOUNTAIN, NORTH CAROLINA 28711

Dedication

To Doctors William and Gladys McGarey
who kindled my interest in this
subject

Disclaimer

There is no intention of the author or the publisher to prescribe for various conditions. We make no claims as to the effect of gemstones on a person's health or other human functions. The purpose for the book is informational - to describe ways in which gemstones were used or suggested to be used, and to gain some understanding of the manner in which they may function. The internal use of powders is particularly cautioned against without consultation with trained medical persons. The manner in which this material is interpreted and used is the sole responsibility of the reader.

*

Biography

The author, Dr. Thelma Isaacs, has unique qualifications to write on this subject. She has B.A. and M.S. degrees in Geology, and a PhD. in Geochemistry and Minerology. Two post-doctoral fellowships (NATO and Leverhulme) followed the awarding of the PhD., and she spent two years doing research and lecturing in Norway and England. She subsequently taught at three universities, and also worked as a materials scientist in an industrial research laboratory where she gained experience in crystal growing and crystallography. She has some 50 publications and 12 patents.

Dr. Isaacs became interested in alternative medicine and holistic health in the mid-1970's, and has studied various aspects of it, including the therapeutic properties of minerals. She has given lectures and workshops, including the 1979 ARE medical symposium.

*

Contents

Introduction

Thousands of years ago, minerals which were and still are gemstones were often used in treating various forms of illness. For reasons as yet unknown, this form of therapy disappeared from the medical scene and the knowledge was essentially lost. Bits and pieces of information (and also misinformation) were carried through time by word of mouth, and, at least in this century, several psychics have referred to this ancient form of therapy in some of their readings.

In recent years, there has been a renewal of interest in what might be called natural healing - that is, healing using natural sources such as massage, herbs, color, sound - rather than drugs, surgery, etc. As we increase our knowledge of the causes of disease and the effects of treatments, and our understanding of life itself, we see that vibrations of various types and frequencies are essential to our existence on this planet. Minerals, which are products of the earth's processes, would be a direct source of vibration. There has developed a growing interest in the ancient art of healing with gemstones. It is probable that the direct application of vibration will be utilized with increasing frequency as we enter into the new age. We need therefore to rediscover old information and, equally, if not more importantly, to expand this knowledge, coordinating it with more recent scientific studies on minerals, both natural and synthetic.

As minerals are a result of geologic processes, an understanding of these phenomena would be of value in developing a knowledge of the subject of healing stones. Internal symmetry, which is reflected in external form, probably also contributes in some way to the effects. Knowledge of geology and symmetry also helps in identification. This book will therefore include some geologic and crystallographic information. In addition, the minerals themselves will be described both chemically and physically.

The information about the therapeutic properties of minerals was gained from a number of sources. My years of experience in minerology, crystal chemistry, crystallography, crystal growth and petrology have given me considerable knowledge of the scientific aspect and contributed to the personal insight which I have developed in this field. Much information was gained from reading books on the subject and from studying the readings of psychics.

Chapters are also included on the theory of the Seven Rays and on synthetic crystals, including speculations about their use in Atlantis, possible future uses, and on understanding the healing properties of gemstones.

*

April 1982   Thelma Isaacs, PhD.

1. Geologic Origins

Minerals, in the strictest sense, are naturally occurring substances which have characteristic internal structures determined by the regular arrangements of the constituent atoms or ions. They have definite chemical compositions and physical properties which may vary within limits. The overwhelming majority are inorganic compounds; a few are native elements. There are also a few organic compounds, but these are relatively unimportant in the overall geology of the crust of the earth. Minerals are the products of the many and varied processes that have been operating within and on the crust of the earth for hundreds of millions of years. They can be formed by crystallization from molten material, solutions, vapor, the interaction of gases and/or liquids with each other and with already existing minerals and rocks. The geologic history of the mineral is that of the rock in which it is found. A knowledge of the formation of rocks therefore gives us a better understanding of minerals and some of their properties. There are three major modes of formation of rock: igneous, sedimentary and metamorphic.

A. Igneous

The term igneous derives from "igneus", the Latin word for fire, and these rocks have a high-temperature origin. They are formed from the solidification of a magma, the molten material formed deep within the crust of the earth, and develop either as intrusive (plutonic) rocks, or are ex-

pelled through fissures in the earth's crust to the
surface as extrusive (volcanic) rocks. The solidification often occurred over a long period of time,
and the various minerals crystallized at different
times during the process. This is particularly the
case for the larger plutonic bodies. The size of
the crystals formed during the cooling is related
to the rate of cooling of the magma. Lavas cool
rapidly, and volcanic rocks are therefore usually
fine-grained or even glassy. Intrusive rocks can
form bodies of various sizes and shapes, and often
there are smaller sub-bodies (off the main one)
produced by the movement of magma through fissures
in surrounding rock during the development process.
These rocks assume a variety of shapes and sizes,
from thin stringers to huge masses thousands of
square kilometers in area. The crystals in the
large, usually deep-seated, plutonic bodies tend to
be of large size as they have large thermal mass
and therefore cool very slowly. Crystals in intermediate and smaller sized intrusives tend to be of
moderate or even small size. Magmas force their
way upward through the overlying rocks either
through fractures or through the strength of their
movement, upwarping the overlying layers. They are
intruded at various depths, with the smaller ones
usually formed at intermediate or shallow depths.

 Igneous rocks not only are classified by
physical origin, but also by mineralogical components which are a reflection of the chemical composition. The principal constituents of a magma
are also the most abundant elements in the crust of
the earth. The most important are oxygen, silicon,
aluminum, iron, magnesium, calcium, sodium, potas-
sium, and hydrogen (the last mentioned usually combined with oxygen to form water). Depending upon
the silica (SiO_2) content, magmas and their corresponding rocks are divided into several groups: ultrabasic, basic, intermediate and acidic - with the
silica content ranging from 40% for the ultrabasic

to 70% for the acidic. There is a corresponding variation for the alkalis, with some magmas (and rocks) being exceptionally rich in soda (Na_2O).

The formation of magma may be due to several factors, the main ones being radioactive processes operating locally, and movement within the crust of the earth causing local melting of the surrounding rocks. Magmas of various compositions can mix or change composition by assimilating rocks through which they pass on their upward migration in the crust. These processes give rise to different types of igneous rocks.

The order of crystallization of the minerals depends upon the original composition of the magma and the conditions under which it crystallizes. The general trend is given by the reaction series of N.L. Bowen, which assumes a basaltic original magma. The left side (which comprises the ferro-magnesian minerals) starts with olivine, which contains discrete tetrahedral groups of SiO_4.

olivine   calcic feldspar

   pyroxene

     hornblende   sodic feldspar

       biotite   potassic feldspar

         muscovite

         quartz

As the temperature drops, and the olivine is in some way removed from participation, the sequence of crystallization proceeds to endless single chains $(Si_2O_6)_n$, then double chains $(Si_4O_{11})_n$, and lastly sheets (Si_4O_{10}), and associates with cations of increasing size. The right-hand side (salic minerals) starts with the crystallization of anorthite $(CaAl_2Si_2O_8)$ and ends with albite $(NaAlSi_3O_8)$ and also contains orthoclase $(KAlSi_3O_8)$. This series represents a compositional change from alkalic to

acidic rocks. In the later stages of crystallization, water and other volatiles play increasingly
important roles. There are also magmas which are
alkalic but are short on calcium and silicon, and
therefore form rocks which are poor in SiO_2; these
are called the under-saturated rocks.

During the later stages of magmatic crystallization, a melt which is rich in volatile constituents remains, and further types of mineral deposits form from it. This melt is very fluid and
can therefore penetrate even fine fissures and cavities in the surrounding rock(s) (which may be the
parent intrusive or country rock), and there deposit minerals which are closely related to those of
the parent rock. These are called pegmatites.
They usually are enriched in the common elements
silicon, aluminum, calcium and alkalis, and also in
a number of uncommon ones such as lithium, beryl-
lium, boron, fluorine, rubidium, cesium, molybdenum,
rare earths, zirconium, hafnium, tantalum, niobium,
thorium, and uranium. Pegmatites usually form in
association with granites or nepheline-syenites and
are formed in the temperature range of 400 - 700°C.
The crystals usually are large (some may weigh several tons) as the volatile constituents act as min-
eralizers. These volatiles can give rise to special
types of mineral deposits which depend upon the temperature of deposition. Above 400°C, they are called pneumatolytic; below that temperature they are
called hydrothermal, as these are deposited from
aqueous solutions. They form veins and fill cavities, and also impregnate existing rock. These
mineral deposits usually form sulphides, selenides
and more rarely tellurides of such elements as iron,
gold, silver, arsenic, molybdenum, nickel, platinum,
copper, zinc, cadmium, mercury, lead, etc. (the sid-
erophilic and chalcophilic elements). Certain oxides, silicates and carbonates of these elements
also may occur.

As the hydrothermal (or hypogene) solutions
move upward through the upper portion of the crust,

they can encounter solutions of surface origin and form deposits of mixed origin.

These late stage deposits (both pneumatolytic and hydrothermal) are the most important sources of many useful minerals containing copper, lead, zinc, cadmium, cobalt, silver, gold, mercury, germanium thallium, molybdenum, etc., and also many useful minerals such as amethyst, aquamarine, topaz, tourmaline, etc.

During the migration of magmatic or pegmatitic melts the country rocks are altered by the introduction or discharge of material from the interaction of the gas or liquid phase with existing minerals. This process, called metasomatism, is one of a volume-for-volume replacement. At the contact between an intrusive and the country rock, certain mineral assemblages (mainly silicates) may be formed, and these are called skarns.

A simplified classification of igneous rocks is given in Table 1, page 6.

*

Existing rocks are usually not stable under surface or near-surface conditions. Rocks undergo weathering, which is the gradual decomposition of unstable minerals (with the disintegration of the rock) and their conversion to other minerals which can persist under these surface conditions. The agents of weathering are both physical and chemical. Physical weathering involves changes of temperature, mechanical action of water, air, etc., and is the predominant mode in cold and dry climates. Here the rocks tend to break up mechanically, or disintegrate. Chemical weathering is produced by living organisms and by surface water and the salts dissolved in them. In warm, humid areas, where there is abundant vegetation and therefore organic acids, the rocks tend to decompose, changing into substances very different in chemical composition

Table 1
Classification of Some Igneous Rocks

Essential minerals	Composition		
	Glassy	Fine Grained	Medium to Coarse Grn.
Acid			
Potassic & sodic feldspar, quartz	obsidian pumice	rhyolite dacite	granite granodiorite
Intermediate			
Sodic to intermediate plagioclase		andesite	diorite
Basic			
Ferromagnesian minerals & calcic plagioclase	basalt-glass	basalt dolorite	gabbro
Ultrabasic			
Calcic plagioclase			anorthosite
Ultrabasic			
Ferromagnesian minerals			peridotite serpentinite dunite
Aberrant Types			
Potassic and sodic feldspar			nepheline-syenite

and physical properties from the original rock.
Chemical weathering includes hydration and hydroly-
sis, oxidation and reduction, carbonization and solution. Most natural waters contain varying amounts
of carbon dioxide, oxygen, nitric oxide, halides,
etc., which enhance their ability to dissolve rocks
and minerals.

Some minerals are more resistant to weathering than others, and may accumulate in local pockets or be carried away by streams and be redeposi-
ted elsewhere. This is how most placer deposits
are formed.

These supergene deposits are formed in con-
tinental areas. There is also only a small-scale
migration of material.

B. Sedimentary

The above contrasts with the formation of
sedimentary deposits which are laid down in water,
and may have been transported over great distances.
They derive from the breaking up and redeposition
of other pre-existing rocks, and also by chemical
precipitation in water and by direct deposition of
organic matter. Sediments may be deposited in seas,
lakes, oceans, flood plains and deltas, and as gla-
cial debris. Because of their mode of formation,
most tend to be layered. Fossils, which are the remains of plants and animals which have been buried,
are often found in sedimentary rocks.

After they are laid down, sediments are converted over time into solid rock. Pressure of overlying sediments brings about compaction (the squee-
zing together of particles), and the precipitation
of such substances as $CaCO_3$ and SiO_2 from aqueous
solutions results in cementation of the particles.

Rocks which are formed from particles of
pre-existing rock are termed clastic, and are classified according to the size of their grains. Where
the grain size is moderate to large (2 mm. and

above), the rock is called a conglomerate. The grain size in sandstone ranges from 1/16 to 1 mm., and in shales and mudstones it is very fine, under 1/16 mm. There may be an interlayering of these types as depositional conditions change, and also they may grade one into another.

Chemically precipitated rocks are classified by composition and mode of origin. The evaporites, mostly salt (NaCl), gypsum ($CaSO_4 \cdot 2H_2O$) and anhydrite ($CaSO_4$) are products of the evaporation of sea water. Chemically precipitated rocks include limestone (chiefly $CaCO_3$), dolomite ($CaMg(CO_3)_2$), and chert (SiO_2). The most important sea minerals are the forms of $CaCO_3$.

The organic rocks are composed primarily of the remains of once-living organisms. Coal, for example, consists of partially decomposed land plants. The most abundant of these organic rocks is limestone, which is made up of fragments of shells or skeletons of animals. Some limestones have been built up by lime-secreting organisms such as algae or coral. There are also clastic limestones composed of fragments of calcareous debris.

There also are rocks which are mixed types: part clastic and part chemical. These would include cherty limestones, clay-limestones, iron formations, black shales, calcareous sandstones, carbonaceous sandstones, etc.

Table 2, page 9 gives a simplified classification of sedimentary rocks.

C. Metamorphic

Already existing rock, within the crust of the earth, may be subjected to conditions of chemical activity, heat and/or pressure, which can effect moderate or even profound changes. They are converted through these processes to metamorphic rocks. The manner and degree of reorganization depends upon the nature of the original rock, the

Table 2
Classification of Sedimentary Rocks

Modified from Gilluly, Waters & Sanford, and
Spock

Clastic Rocks

Rock Type	Major Mineral or Rock Compound	Size of Fragments
Conglomerate	Quartz and rock fragments	Over 2 mm
Breccia	Rock fragments	Over 2 mm
Sandstone		2 to 1/16 mm
Quartz sandstone	Quartz	
	Quartz and feldspar	
	Quartz, feldspar, clay	
	Rock fragments	
Shale	Clay minerals and quartz	Under 1/16 mm
Limestone	Calcite	Variable

Organic and Chemical

Rock Type	Major Mineral or Rock Compound	Chemical Composition
Limestone	Calcite	$CaCO_3$
Dolomite	Dolomite	$CaMg(CO_2)_2$
Peat and coal	Organic matter (plant)	C + hydrocarbons
Chert	Opal, chalcedony	SiO_2 & $SiO_2 \cdot nH_2O$
Evaporites	Halite, gypsum, anhydrite	$NaCl$, $CaSO_4 \cdot 2H_2O$, $CaSO_4$

Mixed Types

Conglomerate	Calcareous	$(CaCO_3)$
Sandstone	Ferruginous	(Fe_2O_3)
Shale	Carbonaceous	(C)
	Argillaceous	(clay)
Limestone	Arenaceous	(sandy)
	Argillaceous	(clay)
	Cherty	(SiO_2)
	Iron formations	(Fe_2O_3)
	Taconite	(Fe_2O_3)
Chert	Ferruginous	(Fe_2O_3)
Shale	Organic matter	(C)

particular metamorphic process, and the intensity
of operation of these influences. These rocks,
while crystalline, did not form from molten material, but rather have undergone changes essentially
without becoming fluid. The main features in their
formation are: partial or complete reorganization
of constituents to form new mineral assemblages;
an increase in grain size to produce coarser textures; and the development of new structures, particularly a parallel arrangement of the minerals.

There are six types of processes operating
in metamorphism. In thermal metamorphism, heat
plays a leading role and the changes are brought
about almost entirely by an increase of temperature. It is essentially a baking process, and is
limited to the immediate vicinity of an igneous
body, either intrusive or extrusive.

When an igneous body has been intruded into
existing rock, there are often emanations, in addition to heat, which can produce changes in mineral composition. Fluids from the magma permeate
the surrounding rocks and may even travel over
considerable distances through them. The new material introduced will change the composition and
mineral assemblage of the host rock. These fluids
may also dissolve and carry away material from the
host rock. This combination of heat and volatile
emanations is called contact metamorphism.

Stresses at moderate depths within the crust
of the earth may build up in localized areas to the
point where rocks are tightly folded and/or sheared
and crushed, resulting in shearing, rolling out and
grinding up of rock and mineral fragments. Real-
ignment of particles without crushing may occur
particularly in the relatively plastic rocks such
as limestone and shale. Chemical change is slight;
the main action is mechanical rearrangement and/or
the crushing of the mineral constituents. This is
termed kinetic metamorphosis.

The most common type of metamorphism is

dynamothermal metamorphism, which includes the combined effects of high temperature and strong, directed pressure. It occurs on a large scale, in zones of intense folding. The rocks thus produced are not only recrystallized, but usually foliated or lineated as well. The main foliated rock-types produced are slates, schists and gneisses, with the degree of recrystallization and mineral change increasing from slate to schist to gneiss. Limestones and sandstones, particularly when fairly pure, do not form foliated rocks, but just recrystallize with the development of a coarser texture. Some new minerals may form from extraneous material within the original rock. Marble and quartzite are typical of these rocks.

Deep within the crust of the earth exist conditions of very high, non-directed pressure and high temperature. This is the zone of plutonic metamorphism. In this zone are produced denser varieties of minerals, and some melting may occur. There is a close association of these rocks with igneous intrusives, and banding, with layers of igneous rock between those of schists or gneiss, may occur. The minerals are anhydrous, or very low in water content.

A sixth type of metamorphism, which is not common, is retrograde metamorphism. It is not a reverse process, but rather one in which metamorphic rocks formed at higher temperatures are later subjected to cooler conditions. The combination of reduced pressure and temperature, coupled with some movement and a supply of water, bring about alterations to a lower grade of metamorphism. Its effects are sporadic and incidental rather than general.

Table 3, page 12 gives a simplified classification of metamorphic rocks.

Table 3
Classification of Metamorphic Rocks
Adapted from Spock

Type of Metamorphosis	Rock Types	Typical Minerals
Thermal	Hornfels Quartzite Marble	Andalusite, grossularite, olivine, wollastonite, anorthite
Contact	Hornfels Quartzite Marble Garnet rocks Ore deposits	Same as thermal plus metal oxides and sulphides
Kinetic	Breccia Granulated rocks Mylonite Some slate	Muscovite, chlorite
Dynamothermal	Phyllite Schist Quartzite Marble	Talc, chlorite, amphiboles, mica, kyanite, garnet, staurolite
Plutonic	Granulite Gneiss Amphibolite Eclogite	Feldspars, garnet, olivite, pyroxenes
Retrograde	Mylonite	Muscovite, talc, chlorite

2. Crystallography

Almost all minerals are crystalline materials; they have definite chemical compositions and regular (ordered) internal arrangements of their constituent atoms, which may be reflected externally by the appearance of plane surfaces (called crystal faces). This occurs when a crystalline solid is allowed to grow unimpeded by external constraints.

A major characteristic of crystals is the property of symmetry. There is order in the arrangement of atoms (and faces) which follows definite patterns. For the sake of clarification, let us consider a tetragonal crystal, as illustrated in Figure 2, page 14. When we look down on top of the crystal, we see that there is a four-fold arrangement of faces about the apex of the pyramid-shaped faces at either end. If we rotate the crystal vertically about this point, we see that the same arrangement of faces is displayed when viewed from the side every 90°. There are four "sets" of identical faces. The line about which rotation takes place is called an axis of symmetry. Here it is a four-fold axis. If we now hold this crystal in such a manner as to rotate it about a horizontal axis cutting two opposite prism faces, we see that the repetition of faces occurs every 180°, or twice during a 360° rotation. This axis shows two-fold symmetry. Further examination shows that each half of the crystal is the mirror image of the other. Also, every face has a similar face lying parallel to it on the opposite side of the crystal (passing through the center of the crystal).

14

This crystal has a center of symmetry.

Not all crystalline materials have the same symmetry elements, but similarly arranged crystals have allied symmetry and may therefore be grouped together. There are seven major groupings or systems based on gross symmetry elements; each of these systems is then divided into subgroups or classes, which are further divided into space groups. For our purposes, we need only consider the major division into systems, and they will be described here, from the highest to the lowest symmetry system.

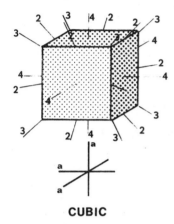

CUBIC

Cubic: Three axes of equal length and mutually perpendicular. In the highest symmetry class there are: 3 axes of 4-fold symmetry. 4 axes of 3-fold symmetry. 6 axes of 2-fold symmetry. 9 planes of symmetry.

Tetragonal: Two axes of equal length, one of a different length, and all mutually perpendicular. In the highest symmetry class there are: 1 axis of 4-fold symmetry. 4 axes of 2-fold symmetry. 5 planes of symmetry.

Hexagonal: Three axes of equal length at 120° from each other, and one axis of unequal length perpendicular to the other three. In

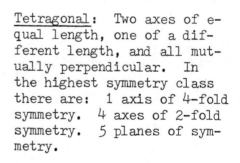

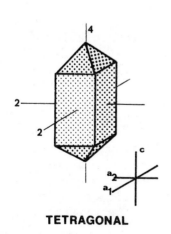

TETRAGONAL

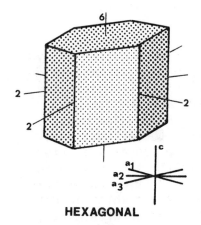

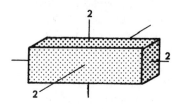

HEXAGONAL

ORTHORHOMBIC

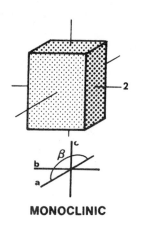

MONOCLINIC

the highest symmetry class there are: 1 axis of 6-fold symmetry. 6 axes of 2-fold symmetry. 7 planes of symmetry.

<u>Trigonal</u>: Sometimes regarded as a sub-group of hexagonal, the main difference being the presence of a three-fold rather than a six-fold principal axis. (There is no drawing). In the highest symmetry class there are: 1 axis of 3-fold symmetry. 3 axes of 2-fold symmetry. 3 planes of symmetry.

<u>Orthorhombic</u>: three axes of unequal length, all perpendicular to each other. In the highest symmetry class there are: 3 axes of 2-fold symmetry. 3 planes of symmetry.

<u>Monoclinic</u>: Three axes of unequal length, two of which are perpendicular to the third, but inclined to one another. In the highest symmetry class there are: 1 axis of 2-fold symmetry. 1 plane of symmetry.

<u>Triclinic</u>: Three axes of unequal length and inclined to each other at

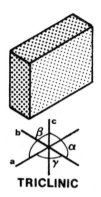

TRICLINIC

different angles.

The presence or absence of a center of symmetry can be of importance particularly for certain device applications. In some instruments (e.g., radar), the crystal must have the property of piezo-electricity, which means that only crystals of certain classes which do not have a center of symmetry can be considered. Certain other properties (e.g., pyro-electricity, second harmonic generation, electro-optic) also will be found only in crystals which are non-centrosymmetric. Other physical properties such as cleavage (breaking along smooth, plane surfaces usually in a particular direction) are a reflection of the internal atomic arrangement.

3. Theory Of The Seven Rays

The philosophy behind this doctrine is that there are seven rays of life (or types of forces), one of which dwells in every form whether it be animate or so-called inanimate. Precious stones have special properties which enable them to act as wave-meters, transmitting specialized psychic qualities.

In occult science, each particle, whether it be organic or inorganic, is a life connected with the Supreme Being called God. There is thus the same life-pulse behind each particle, even though the forms are different. In occult philosophy, "there is a place for the mineral kingdom in the great sweeping outlines of the evolutionary scheme, not only granting it an indwelling life, but chronicling the earlier stages of life now dreaming in the minerals of our planet and forecasting its immensely remote future" (Stewart, p. 21).

There is the theory in occult science that the sun outlasts a set of planets, and that it can have (and probably has had) more than one such set. There are areas where special evolutionary work is carried on in historical continuity from an old planet to a new one. Preliminary work and also finishing work are carried out in physically invisible planets, in materials which are far more sensitive than is physical matter. From the earliest stages there were will and life inherent in the atoms, but the life which evolves towards higher forms comes in great pulses or waves at very long time intervals. It first dwells in invisible

worlds where form can hardly bind it and in its
desire for clear contact with an external world,
works its way slowly into denser forms of matter.
It enters the physical world where it is tied
down in the mineral. In this state it is faintly
aware of violent physical impacts such as earth-
quakes, volcanoes, water, fire, electricity and
even human activity. Vibrations from these acti-
vities are sent to the life within, so that in the
course of many years it becomes dimly conscious of
a something outside itself and goes on to the next
cycle of a humble form of plant. These events occur with the help of intelligences other than the
Supreme Mind, which come from other solar systems.
A further belief is that the moon is a predecessor
of the earth (moons are bodies of the ancestor of
the new planet). The life that expresses itself
through our mineral kingdom was the third elemental kingdom of the moon. It was astral in its material rather than physical.

There are seven successive pulses or life-
waves running parallel on the earth and the oldest
is that in which human beings are carried along.
There are also the animal, vegetable, mineral, and
three elemental kingdoms. There is a long period
of rest following each stage. Following the rest
period from the lunar evolution there began the
preliminary work for our present system, or round.
The earth system has seven "globes" (labelled A
through G), the earth itself being in the mid-pos-
ition (D). We are presently in the fourth of sev-
en rounds. The mineral kingdom was formed on the
last globe of the first round, and everything that
exists in this kingdom was formed at that time, although formed only in filmy shapes.

There is a systematic development in each
round. On globe A arise the seven archetypal
forms for each kingdom which multiply forms containing the essentials of each on globe B. These
forms densify on globe C, and are shaped into ever

denser matter on globe D. On globe E, they become
more complex and refined, and are further refined
on globe F. They are perfected on globe G.

The life-pulse of the mineral kingdom comes
from outside this cosmic-prakritic plane; it is a
manifestation of the Divine Force. The subject is
complex in good part because of the parallel evolution. We must remember that the life-pulse in
its evolution towards humanity manifests first
through the elemental kingdom and then through the
mineral kingdom. These two bodies at these different stages are in manifestation at the same time;
one (the earth elemental) occupies the same space
as and inhabits the other (e.g., a rock), but this
does not in any way interfere with the evolution
of either, nor does it imply any relation between
the bodies of life-pulse lying within both. Each
will also be permeated by a totally distinct and
individual variety of the omni-present life-prin-
ciple.

Precious stones are part of the mineral
kingdom and some of them have a vibration which
naturally corresponds with the vibration rates of
some of the higher emotions. The particles of
these minerals move naturally on the physical plane
tuned to a key which is identical at this lower
level with the key of purity on higher levels. It
will act as a check upon impure thoughts or feelings by virtue of its overtones, and can readily
be charged at either the astral or mental levels
with vibrations of pure thought or feeling which
are in the same key. The gemstone represents the
highest development of the mineral kingdom and
thus has much greater power of receiving and retaining impressions than most other objects. The
Gnostic gems used in initiation ceremonies were
(and still are) strong centers of magnetic influence.

Another factor in their effectiveness is
that many precious stones have permanent atoms

attached to them. "A permanent atom is a special
atom linked to a little pool of divine life which
one day becomes the spirit of man" (Stewart, p.27).
Every human body contains one, which has been in
each of the bodies worn during every incarnation,
and large numbers of these special atoms are also
distributed in the various forms of living matter
all about us. Each of these atoms will in some
future time become the nucleus of a human being.

The occult scientist, as an investigator and
observer of the forces and structures of superphy-
sical regions, regards the three origins of rocks
as representing the qualities of the first, second
and third Logos (the three Persons of the Trinity).
The division which is of most importance to present
day human beings is that of the Seven Rays. "It
places each man in rapport with sections of the
manifested world below and above him" (Stewart,
p. 31). Each ray contains a part of universal
(God) consciousness, and in each of the Ray divi-
sions (the Seven Rays of the One Light) are found
members of all of the both visible and invisible
natural kingdoms. Each of the life-pulses contains
all seven types. There is a consonance or disson-
ance of vibrational rates between man and natural
objects which is not usually of a high strength,
but which accumulates power when acting over long
periods of time. The soil and rock over which one
lives may well have a long-term physical and also
psychic effect. (Perhaps this is a factor behind
the recommendation of Edgar Cayce to drink the water and eat the vegetables and fruits of the area
in which one is currently living to better accli-
mate to the area.)

The Rays are deliberately numbered in such
a way that natural relationships are maintained.
The first three Rays (the major Rays) have in themselves the qualities of the Trinity (will, wisdom
and creative activity).

The First Ray is distinguished by the will;
its children show it as their supreme quality

through courage, strength, inflexibility and the ability to appreciate the value of each individual. It is the Ray of the born warrior and/or ruler. Its methods are direct; it represents the Power of God. The diamond, the hardest and most brilliant of natural gemstones, is its highest development in the mineral kingdom. Its color is electric-blue.

The Second Ray type is the love which is wisdom. It is the great teaching Ray reflecting the unity and interdependence of all that lives. Its children have a nobility which springs from heart-wisdom and unselfish love. It is the Ray of great religious figures such as the Buddha and the Christ. The color is indigo.

The Third Ray is that of creative activity and corresponds to the third person (Holy Spirit) of the Trinity. It knows the materials and calculates the stresses they can stand, their best arrangement in space, and other factors in "construction". Its members tend to see a situation in the entirety. They may be engineers, judges, philosophers, town planners, etc. The Third Ray has green as its color. This Ray acts as a director and focus for the remaining four rays.

The Fourth Ray has a both human and exhilarating atmosphere about it. Children of this Ray seek harmony and are intuitively aware of the glorious rhythm and balance maintained throughout the evolving universe. They are endowed by spiritual birth as potential creators of beauty and harmony. Leonardo daVinci was a Fourth Ray person. Orange is the color of this Ray.

The Fifth Ray person also is seeking order in the universe around him, but his ideal is stability and form (rather than rhythm and life of the Fourth Ray). The person of this Ray prefers to omit the personal equation and to study objects by objects. This is the Ray of concrete science and ordered knowledge (left-brain thinking). Its color is golden yellow.

The Sixth Ray represents utter devotion to a divine personality or even to an abstract ideal. All the forces of a human being can be brought together for a lifetime of sustained effort by this Ray. There is a basic sympathy between it and the Second Ray. The Second Ray person feels divine love in a sweet and impersonal way, while the Sixth Ray person longs for a direct relationship between God and him/herself. The young Krishna and Jesus Christ personify this Ray. Its color is crimson or rose-red. This Ray was the dominant one in Western Europe for many centuries, until the early 1800's.

The Seventh Ray, which is succeeding the Sixth as dominant in the world, is the ceremonial Ray, as it is characterized by beauty and purpose in skilled action. It borrows the essence of all rays and the developed person of this Ray devises a scheme of action which is precise, logical, harmonious and economical. This person is very much aware of psychological and psychic factors, and utilizes the forces of invisible worlds by ceremonies as well as constructing objects on the material plane. Contact can be made on this line with the Devas. Freemasonry and its allied movements are social organisms of this Ray. This Ray has particular connections with the mineral kingdom which uses its magic. There is also another Seventh Ray type less positive in nature, who is sensitive to nature and the nature spirits (Devas). This type would be the rare literary genius and the prime musician. The color of the Ray is violet.

It must be noted that the true colors of the Rays are seldom given out, and also that in passing from one plane to another they are liable to be reversed into their complementary colors.

It is difficult to ascertain one's own Ray as that of the inner person is frequently not evident in the accomplishments of the transient personality. In religious ceremonies, precious stones are foci through which the special energies of the various Rays may be conducted by Deva helpers to stimulate worship in the congregation.

4. Healing Gemstones

A. Use Of Healing Gemstones

There are two principal ways in which gemstones have been utilized in healing: external
and internal. Generally they are worn on the body,
either directly touching the skin or in a setting
of precious metal (silver or gold) and worn as jewelry. They may be placed on the affected area of
the body, or on one of the chakras. They may be
held in the hand and fingered (rubbed), rubbed on
the affected part of the body, and perhaps also
rubbed on appropriate acupressure points. They may
also be used as "lenses" transmitting light and
other forms of energy to plants or animals.
    Healing stones have also been used inter-
nally in a number of ways. In Europe during the
Middle Ages, they were pulverized and small amounts
of the powder were ingested, usually in some liquid
(often wine). One wonders if they can be potenti-
zed in a manner similar to homeopathic medicines,
and their vibrations thereby increased, and then
taken homeopathically. Ayurvedic physicians in
India use the ashes of gemstones (which have been
burned in a special process or pulverized) to prepare some of their medicines. The theory behind
this practice is that the rays emitted by these
ashes are akin to isotopes. A less expensive way
to use gemstones medicinally is to place a stone in
liquid (pure water or alcohol) for several days and
then drink this liquid. The liquid becomes charged
with the vibrations of the mineral. One recommendation is to place a gemstone in a glass vial con-

taining a diluted alcohol solution, and place this in a dark area for a week to allow time for the vibratory forces of the gem to permeate the solution. The gem is then removed, washed and dried, and reserved for further use. As the sun has healing properties and the full spectrum of light plus other vibrations is useful, perhaps putting the glass container with the gemstone in sunlight would enhance some of the effects. In color therapy, glass bottles of different colors are filled with water and exposed to the sun; and the water contained in them is then drunk. Each of the colors has a different effect.

Gemstones are sometimes worn in the form of talismans. The underlying theory was that the healing properties inherent in these stones would be enhanced when they were engraved with a symbol or figure possessing special qualities. These figures were believed to impart to the wearer the qualities associated with them, and were supposed to have efficacy in themselves independent of the powers of the mineral on which they were engraved. Various factors entered into their efficacy including the vibrations of the mineral, of the carver, the form of the talisman, the hour, day and month during which this work was done. (The influence of the planet, star or constellation which was then in the ascendent was thought to exert a subtle influence on the stone while the carving was being performed.) For maximum power, it was thought that the properties of the image should be the same as those inherent in the material. The wearer of the talisman also contributes his/her vibrations.

Lama Sing states that talismans can be a burden as well as a blessing, and mentions some beneficial and detrimental forms. He further mentions that some rocks (e.g., granite, basalt, and other common rocks) are quite stable, and if used in their native state (unpolished) can affect a stabilizing influence. They are not used as they are not con-

sidered aesthetically pleasing. Minerals which
are ores of iron, nickel, copper, silver, gold, ti-
tanium, uranium, phosphorus, etc., differ somewhat
from rocks in that they are in graduated levels of
change or alteration and therefore are not so stable as rocks. He believes that the beneficial talismans "are largely those which denote in the mental form and spiritual form of the bearer or wearer
that which relates to that spiritual-mental purpose
in the earth plane". The fish denotes warmth to
many people, particularly to those who have some
recall of experiences in Essene communities following the birth of Jesus, to those who were fisher-
men in Atlantis, and to those who built harmonious
relationships between distant tribes in Og and Mu.
The cross, which is the symbol of light, can have
its effects heightened when present with the fish;
it denotes wonder of the Master's presence and intense love. The pyramid is effective particularly
with a star within its perimeter. The Star of David, often containing a cross within it (Gothic or
Coptic cross using multiple cross-bars), can have
a significant effect. A simple circle or sphere
is effective, and may be heightened somewhat by
having the true birth sign emblazoned upon it. The
triangle or pyramid which contains a small turquoise in its center is also good. The alpha and
omega of the Greek alphabet are also good, especially if made of wood or of favorable metals or
minerals. When these symbols are made from a porous material such as wood, they tend to be receivers; when made from dense hard substances, they
tend to be transmitters, although they also receive
on very specific levels. He recommends using native minerals (nuggets or crystals). He further
suggests that one depend upon one's own inner know-
er for other symbols.

These are all tools to aid in one's progres-
sion with the oneness of God. Lama Sing warns a-
gainst using numerical figures, particularly when
made of metal. There is a tendency here to inten-

sify a certain level of energy, and the metal may
vibrate in relationship with it and bring about
problems. Inverted pyramids can deplete a person's
energies (by focussing too much on the physical
form) and should not be worn. The inverted cross
also is to be avoided as it signifies general in-
tents not beneficial to spiritual consciousness.
The Star of David should not be made of wood as it
may then absorb too much of the attitudes of the
people with whom they are related. This symbol
should be made of a non-porous substance (mineral
or rock). The cross, however, is just the opposite
in that it should preferentially be of wood, especially if made by the wearer. Other detrimental
forms are half or quarter moons enblazoned upon a
disc which also has a variety of stones at its cir-
cumference.

In the following pages, thirty gemstones or
groups of stones and metals are described, with
their healing properties gleaned from numerous
sources. There often is not good agreement as to
their effects and one reason may be that psychic
readings were given for individuals and the same
gemstone may not have the same effects on different
people. Also, with much of the ancient lore for-
gotten and no records as yet discovered, psychics
and others are only picking up pieces of information. Much of the information that has been passed
down (and often found in various writings of al-
chemists, scholars, etc.) through folklore and/or
other sources is bastardized and probably incor-
rect. It is based on insufficient or false information, superstition, exaggeration and even chica-
nery and greed. The reasons for the uses of these
minerals are lost in antiquity; they probably go
back to pre-history, to Atlantis. The therapeutic
efficacy of gemstones is therefore an almost unknown phenomenon today. Perhaps our "best" current
information is to be found in the readings of 20th
century psychics such as Edgar Cayce. Another

factor to consider is the probably frequent mis-
identification of minerals and gemstones in the
past, making it difficult to know which properties
are properly ascribed to which stones.

B. Descriptive Properties

It has been said that some gemstones have
the property of being able to predict danger or
serious illness by fading or changing color and becoming dull and lifeless. These stones are reputed
to be sensitive to physical and atmospheric disturbances, and there are many legends about them.

*

Disclaimer: There is no intention in these pages
to prescribe for various conditions. The purpose
for their writing is informational - to describe
the way in which gemstones and precious metals were
used in the past or are suggested to be used. The
internal use of powders is particularly cautioned
against without consultation with properly trained
medical persons. The author does not recommend or
prescribe such use, nor the use of stones externally. The manner in which this material is interpreted and used is the responsibility of the reader.

*

Two properties, hardness and density, are
used in identification of minerals. Hardness of a
substance is its resistivity to the scratching of
a smooth surface and is dependent upon the bonding
of the constituent atoms within the crystal structure. The relative degree of hardness can be determined by the comparative ease (or difficulty)
with which one material can be scratched by another. A harder material will leave a furrow (or
scratch) on a softer one. The pressure applied by

the harder substance causes the breaking up of the
atomic bonds on a microscopic scale. A reference
scale of ten common minerals was established by
Friedrich Mohs who arranged them in order of increasing hardness in the following scale:

1.	Talc	6.	Feldspar
2.	Gypsum	7.	Quartz
3.	Calcite	8.	Topaz
4.	Fluorite	9.	Corundum
5.	Apatite	10.	Diamond

This scale is approximately linear from 1 through
8; starting at 9, the curve steepens markedly.

Density or specific gravity is a number
which expresses the ratio of the weight of a material compared to that of an equal volume of water
at $4°C$. Density is a function of a number of factors, the main ones being chemical composition and
crystal structure.

Amber

Composition: $C_{10}H_{16}O + H_2S$

Crystallography: Amorphous

Form: Massive

Hardness: 2 - 2.5

Density: 1.05 - 1.096

Cleavage and Fracture: Conchoidal fracture

Color: Yellow, brown, reddish, cream, orangish.

Occurrance: Amber is the hardened resin of pine trees and is approximately thirty million years old. Inclusions, usually insects or pollen, are common; they were trapped in the viscous, sticky fluid as it oozed from the trees. It is sometimes found in sedimentary deposits, having been transported by streams.

Healing Properties: Amber has long been prized as a gem. It was regarded as a charm to be used against disease and infection. A volatile oil can be distilled from it and this oil was believed to be useful in treating infantile convulsions. When ground up with honey and rose oil and ingested, it was a treatment for deafness, ear ache, and poor sight. Powdered amber, alone or with other substances, was applied to burns, ulcers and carbuncles to aid in healing. When added to water, it was used to treat ague, dysentary, stomach pains, and to activate the liver and kidneys. The Chinese also used powdered amber in many of their medicines. The area of the throat was the major body area to which amber was applied, and amber necklaces have been prescribed for such conditions as goitre, catarrh, ulcers, soreness, hay fever, growths and asthma. It was also worn about the neck to calm the nerves.

In Muslim nations, it was valued for incense as well as a talisman. Amber is a gem of the Fifth Ray.

Azurite
(Lapis Linguis)

Composition: $Cu_3(CO_3)_2(OH)_2$

Crystallography: Monoclinic

Form: Azurite may form small well-developed crystals exhibiting many forms; it also occurs in stalactitic or earthy aggregates, massive, banded.

Hardness: 3.5 - 4

Density: 3.77

Cleavage and Fracture: One perfect cleavage. Fracture conchoidal, brittle.

Color: Azure to dark blue

Occurrence: Azurite is a sedimentary mineral formed by the action of bicarbonate solutions on primary copper sulphides. It often alters to malachite and may be mixed with it.

Healing Properties: In the readings of Edgar Cayce, azurite was believed to help those with psychic talents to develop these abilities. It also increases attunements to higher forces. There is the problem of identification in a number of his readings, however, and this may have been, at least in part, the mineral referred to as lapis lazuli (see Lazurite). It is possible that some of the therapeutic properties of azurite have been attributed to lazurite by him.

Paul Solomon has stated that azurite is of value in stimulating visual impulses during meditation and in clarifying dreams. He recommended

wearing the mineral in the center of the forehead
for greater effect. He felt that this was the
practice of the priests in ancient Egypt. In other
readings, he mentioned that azurite would be of as-
sistance in developing self-communication. He and
Tracy Johnson believe that it and (probably) malachite would be better for healing than lazurite
(which is more of a spiritual stone).

Richardson/Huett state that azurite is a
light stone and therefore a good one to be used by
the neophyte, particularly in meditation. It has
a light cleaning or purifying spiritual effect, and
a gentle love aspect. Its effects are mainly sur-
ficial as it does not have strong vibrations. They
suggest wearing it in a ring on the right hand; it
also can be used as a focal point in meditation by
holding two (silver dollar sized) pieces in the
hands.

There are some who think that azurite was
used in Atlantis and ancient Egypt, and that it was
one of the most potent of all the gemstones both
for healing and for spiritual attunement. It may
have had secret influences as its past use is
shrouded in mystery. Some of the influences may
have been of a sinister nature; some healing gems
(particularly the strong ones) can become very negative in effect if used for the wrong purposes.
Perhaps its effects were deliberately held secret
by the priests to keep people from misusing the
stone.

Beryl
(Aquamarine & Emerald)

Composition: $Be_3Al_2Si_6O_{18}$
Emerald has a trace of Cr^{3+} substituting for Al.
Aquamarine may have traces of Fe^{2+}, V, Mn, Fe^{3+}
substituting for Al.

Crystallography: Hexagonal

Form: Crystals are usually prismatic, elon-
gated or flattened, equant; often striated or etch-
ed; massive.

Hardness: 7.5 - 8

Density: 2.65 - 2.9

Cleavage and Fracture: One poor cleavage.
Parting indistinct.

Dispersion: Low

Color: Green, pinkish, yellow to yellowish-
orange, red, blue

Occurrence: Beryl is a pegmatitic mineral
and is found in granitic rocks and schists. It is
also concentrated in placer deposits.

Healing Properties: Edgar Cayce suggested
that beryl in general would be a good stone for
protection and for greater receptivity.

Aquamarine: Tracy Johnson recommends aquamarine
to help give purpose and direction and self-under-
standing, to give strength and tranquility to the
emotional, mental and physical body to become better attuned to the Creative Forces. She suggested
wearing it in a pendant.

Richardson/Huett believe that this is an excellent stone for meditation, but that it has little in the way of healing properties. It has a mild effect on the thymus in that it softens the opening of the heart center, and is therefore best worn as a necklace or pendant over the thymus gland.

In ancient times, aquamarine was thought to banish fear and protect the wearer from poisons. The Romans believed it would cure illnesses of the stomach, liver, jaws and throat. In the Middle Ages, it was believed to render the wearer unconquerable, quicken his intelligence, and cure laziness.

Emerald: Both Tracy Johnson and Paul Solomon indicate that the green color of emerald has much to do with its healing properties and recommend this gemstone for quieting the emotions, balancing the aura, and for healing.

Lama Sing believes that the emerald has the quality of amplification, particularly relating to the pineal - pituitary glands (see Ruby).

Richardson/Huett consider emerald to be a remarkable stone with unlimited future potential. It has great spiritual value in that it has the effect of enhancing wisdom from the mental plane. It also has a strong love vibration. Physically, it strengthens the heart and spine, and helps alleviate problems associated with sugar diabetes, and also stimulates the adrenal glands. Its effects are more upon the chakras than the glands; it causes each center to feel its own purpose and being, particularly in the area of the solar plexus. The moon and its phases affect this stone, and it is best used when the moon is full.

Other therapeutic uses for emerald include: as an antidote for poisons, treatment for diseases of the eyes, promoting functional activity of the liver, protection against possession by demons, protection of travellers, enhancing memory and

mental powers, eloquence, clairvoyance, cure for
epilepsy, and lessening pains of childbirth. The
main use of the emerald in ancient and medieval
times was in treating eye diseases, especially inflammations. Sometimes the stones would be steeped
in water for several hours or days, and the infu-
sion then used to bathe the eyes. Powders dissolved in water or other medications were also used as
eye lotions. In some ancient societies, it was a
symbol of Spring and a guardian of the processes of
generation and ripening.

Aquamarine and emerald are gemstones of the
Third Ray.

Chrysoberyl

Composition: $BeAl_2O_4$

Crystallography: Orthorhombic

Form: Crystals are usually tabular. Twinning is common and forms pseudo-hexagonal crystals.

Hardness: 8.5

Density: 3.68 - 3.73

Cleavage and Fracture: Two cleavages: one good, the other poor. Fracture conchoidal. Brittle.

Color: Yellow, yellowish green, grey, blue-green, brown, green, red, violet. In alexandrite (which contains a small amount of Cr^{3+} replacing Al), the color varies with light, being green or blue-green in daylight and mauve, violet to red or purplish in incandescent light. Catseye is usually dark yellowish-brown to pale yellow, honey yellow, greenish.

Dispersion: Low

Occurrence: Chrysoberyl is usually found in granites, pegmatites and aplites. It also occurs in mica schists.

Healing Properties: According to Richardson/Huett, the healing qualities of chrysoberyl are on the emotional (astral) and mental planes, bringing peace of mind to the wearer. It particularly affects the heart center and helps bring charity to the heart of the person wearing the stone. It has a subtle but persistent vibration.

It may also lightly stimulate the adrenal glands.
Wearing the stone in the navel or over the solar
plexus area for short periods of time is recommended in this connection.

Chrysoberyl is not much mentioned as a healing gemstone elsewhere. It is a newer stone and
may not therefore have been considered centuries
ago. One can speculate that its effects may be similar to beryl when the stone is clear. Catseye may
have a strengthening and stabilizing influence, and
may also help with intellectual endeavors.

In Russia (before the revolution), alexandrite was thought to be a good omen for the wearer.

In Ceylon, it has been used as a charm a-
gainst evil spirits.

Chrysocolla

Composition: $(Cu,Al)_2H_2Si_2O_5(OH)_4 \cdot nH_2O$

Crystallography: Orthorhombic

Hardness: 2 - 4; as high as 7 if highly silicified.

Density: 2.40 - 2.42

Cleavage and Fracture: No cleavage; fracture conchoidal. Very brittle, especially if not silicified.

Colors: Blue, green, bluish-green; also brown and black when oxides of calcium, iron and manganese are present.

Occurrence: Chrysocolla is formed by the action of ground water on copper-bearing minerals under oxidizing conditions. It often is mixed with sedimentary colloidal silica forming a gel which hardens to a blue material which is essentially a chalcedony saturated with chrysocolla. It may be mixed with malachite.

Healing Properties: Chrysocolla is included because there is speculation that it may have been the mineral Edgar Cayce meant when he referred to lapis lazuli. (See the section on lazurite for further discussion.) Chrysocolla has not been called a healing stone elsewhere, and its therapeutic potential is uncertain. Chrysocolla is a very brittle mineral, particularly if not well-silicified, and therefore does not lend itself well to cutting and polishing. This factor would militate against its having been much used in the past as a healing stone. It may have similar properties to other copper-bearing minerals.

Copper

Composition: Cu

Crystallography: Cubic

Form: Crystals are rare, and in cubic or dodecahedral form. Usually massive filiform or arborescent.

Hardness: 2.5 - 3

Density: 8.94

Cleavage and Fracture: No cleavage; fracture hackly.

Color: Copper

Occurrence: Native copper is formed by the action of secondary copper-bearing solutions upon iron-bearing minerals such as hematite, or when copper-bearing solutions interact with ferrous or ferric sulphate solutions in the supergene zone of copper sulphide deposits. It is generally associated with basic extrusive igneous rocks.

Healing Properties: In a reading, Edgar Cayce mentioned that copper would enhance emotional release to aid in attunement between the spiritual and the mental. Lama Sing suggests that copper affects the blood and the purity of the body and is therefore useful for "fluidic" problems. This is accomplished by an increased rate of frequency of vibrations which affects the movement of the molecular structure of fluids.

Richardson/Huett state that copper has the ability to draw off the dregs of many things within the body by oxidizing through the pores. It is predominently useful in ridding the body of excesses of metallic impurities, particularly manganese.

In recent years, copper has been worn (usually in bracelets) to help in the healing of arthritis. The results, thus far, have been mixed.

Coral

Composition: $CaCO_3$ (composed primarily of calcite).

Crystallography: Trigonal

Form: Cluster or colony

Hardness: 3.5 - 4

Density: 2.6 - 2.7

Cleavage and Fracture: No cleavage

Color: White, pink, rose red, red to dark red.

Occurrence: Coral consists of the axial skeleton of a marine animal called the coral polyp. It is a tiny, almost plant-like, animal that inhabits warm oceans, and lives in colonies. The solid material called coral is this colony.

Healing Properties: Cayce recommended wearing coral to raise a person's vibrations to better attune oneself to nature and creative forces. It was to be worn against the flesh rather than decoratively. Tracy Johnson suggests that wearing pink immature coral about the neck would aid in achieving tranquility.

Plato recommended that children wear coral about their necks and also that it be rubbed on their gums to prevent epilepsy.

Other powers attributed to coral include averting the fell spell of the evil eye, staunching the flow of blood from an open wound, curing madness, giving wisdom. Red coral was thought to be a remedy against melancholy. In the Middle Ages, it was used medicinally as an astringent, a heart stimulant, and as a remedy for poisoning and fevers. When pulverized with pearl, it was used to treat colic and vomiting. In ancient Rome, the ashes were used in salves for ulcers, scars, and sore eyes. Ayurvedic ashes, when ingested, have been claimed to be helpful in a number of areas, such as asthma, obesity, anemia, jaundice, eye troubles, urinary tract diseases, constipation, fevers, indigestion, loss of appetite, cough, emaciation and rickets, and increase of beauty.

Brown corals are reputed to be attractive to evil spirits. In the Orient, mystics warn against wearing dull, dirty or discolored specimens. There is also a belief that coral must not be washed in order to retain its powers as an amulet.

Coral has tentatively been called a gemstone of the Sixth Ray.

Corundum
(Ruby & Sapphire)

Composition: Al_2O_3. Ruby has a trace of Cr^{3+} replacing Al. Sapphire usually has a trace of Fe^{3+} or Ti^{3+} replacing Al.

Crystallography: Trigonal

Form: Crystals are commonly tabular to short prismatic. They may also be steep pyramidal, rough rounded barrel-shaped, and also massive granular.

Hardness: 9

Density: 4.05

Cleavage and Fracture: No cleavage; one parting often displayed on natural mineral.

Color: Ruby: pinkish red, medium to dark red. Sapphire: light to dark blue, pink, green, colorless, yellow.

Dispersion: low

Occurrence: Corundum is usually formed through a desilication of pegmatitic solutions as they percolate through ultrabasic rocks. It also can be a result of thermal or regional metamorphism of sedimentary rocks rich in aluminum.

Healing Properties:
Ruby: Edgar Cayce suggested that the ruby would be an aid to mental concentration and a bringer of strength to the wearer. The readings of Paul Solomon and Tracy Johnson recommend it as a helpful focus of the vital life energies. Johnson

also suggested holding the stone in the left hand
in quiet moments or while listening to music, as
well as wearing it. She recommended that they not
be worn continuously over a period of time.

In one of his readings, Lama Sing commented
that rubies (and emeralds) amplify generally in a
spectrum relating to the pineal-pituitary glands.
They are used largely by those who have fluidic
difficulties in terms of talismans; it is a sort
of amulet which purifies the blood (the fluidic
part of the body). Its effects are strongly mental and it is probably inadvisable to wear them
when under severe emotional or mental challenge, as
the amplification would be too much for the person.
It is a valuable crystal for the gathering and amplification of energies, and it also can have a
small effect on the electrochemical balance of the
body, and can tend to reduce epidermal enzymes.
It is generally best used by persons of low density vibrations.

According to Richardson/Huett, ruby aids in
the circulation of blood and in cleansing the blood
of infection. When used in conjunction with a
prism, it can aid in dissolving blood clots. It
can also strengthen the adrenal glands through the
purification of the blood and stabilize the eyes.
Spiritually, it reflects the quality of love and
would be useful as a meditation stone for those
who are lacking in self-love. It is also a stone
of spiritual courage.

The ruby was probably the most valued gemstone by the Hindus; it is called "ratnaraj" (king
of precious stones) and "ratnanayaks" (leader of
precious stones). Many believe that the ruby is
best worn on the left side of the body or left
hand. It was thought to protect the wearer from
adversity, to guard his house and possessions from
storms in ancient times. It also has been used to
treat snakebite, fever, ailments of the blood, kidneys and liver, to staunch the flow of blood when

ground up and mixed with water or medicines and used as a paste. To dream of a ruby indicated success. In medieval times, the ruby was thought to have the power of curing or enabling the wearer to forget evils springing from friendship or love. It is one of the seven precious substances of Buddhism. Ayurvedic physicians use the ashes for tuberculosis, pain, colic, boils, ulcers, poisoning, eye troubles, and constipation. In India, rubies are sometimes taped to the forehead to influence the thoughts, or placed under the pillow to induce pleasant dreams. It may have a beneficial effect on the blood. In the East, it is thought to bring about contentment, and also good health, long life and enduring happiness.

The ruby is a gemstone of the Sixth Ray.

The ruby is used as a laser crystal. It has properties which enable it to store energy and then release it in a burst.

Sapphire: Only brief mention is made of the sapphire by Solomon and Johnson, and none by Cayce. The blue color seems of importance to Solomon and Johnson; the latter indicated that it would be of more help to those of quiet attitudes and natures.

Richardson/Huett state that the sapphire brings lightness and joy and also a depth of beauty and thoughts to the wearer. It is best worn as a ring set in silver to emit healing vibrations. When worn as a pendant, it can draw negative forces from other people. The blue stone is preferable for healing; the black worn for protection or as a centering stone for the body. The white sapphire can act as a focal point to center the mind, and is of high spiritual quality. The star sapphire works mainly on the chakras of the etheric body, while the clear blue works on the mental body. The sapphire has its own vibrations which work independently of the energies of the wearer.

Various beliefs have existed about the properties of the sapphire. It was believed to be a

protector against enchantments, an enemy to black
choler, to free the mind and mend manners, to make
the wearer devout and chaste, to obviate bleeding
from piles, and to remove catarrh with sore throats.
It was also thought to be a powerful influence for
purity and continence, and is therefore used in ec-
clesiastical rings of bishops and cardinals of the
Catholic Church.

Sapphire was a much respected stone by the
Buddhists, who ascribed sacred magical power to it.
They believe that it produces peace of mind, equa-
nimity, and chases all evil thoughts by establish-
ing a healthy circulation in man. It will open bar-
red doors and dwellings (for the spirit of man) and
produces a desire for prayer. The person who would
wear it must lead a pure and holy life. Ayurvedic
physicians use the ashes of the sapphire to treat
rheumatism, colic and mental illness.

Some of the properties claimed for the sapphire may have been those of lazurite. There was a
tendency many years ago to transfer the properties
of one stone of a particular color to another of
similar color and higher monetary value. The sapphire may have been one of the gemstones set in the
breastplate of the High Priests.

It is a gemstone of the Second Ray.

Diamond

Composition: C

Crystallography: Cubic

Form: Commonly octahedral, dodecahedral, cubic or tetrahedral; two or more faces often occur in combination resulting in curved faces.

Hardness: 10. The hardest natural substance. (Interestingly enough, the other form of carbon, graphite, is one of the softest minerals.)

Density: 3.515

Cleavage and Fracture: One excellent cleavage.

Dispersion: High

Colors: Colorless, grey, yellow, brown, pink, green, lavender, blue, black. The clear colorless and blue-white diamonds are the ones of interest in healing, although some of the "fancies" (clear colored stones) may well also be of value.

Occurrence: Diamonds are found in an ultrabasic igneous rock called kimberlite and are formed under conditions of great pressures and high temperatures which occur at considerable depth within the crust of the earth. The material is then exploded in fissures in overlying rocks to a new surface position. Diamonds are also found in placers in the stream gravels. Small diamonds, formed by the heat and pressure of impact, have been found in some meteorites.

Healing Properties: Diamonds are mentioned

in several readings by Edgar Cayce to "bring vibratory reactions and experiences in the environs of
the entity" and to keep the vibrations of the body
in better attunement with infinity rather than with
the purely mental or material aspects of life. In
one reading, he stated that it is a selfish stone,
and its misuse can bring about irritation to the
wearer, but if used unselfishly, it can bring
peace.

Richardson/Huett state that the diamond is
best used in conjunction with other stones as its
healing properties are not of a specific nature.
It has the ability to enhance the effects of other
stones, and is particularly helpful when used with
emerald and amethyst. It enhances the energies of
body, mind and spirit. It also aids in opening the
two highest centers (third eye and crown), and can
be used to attune the entity to higher forces.

Diamonds have been used for general healing.
Taken internally - either pulverized and mixed with
liquid, or more commonly steeped in water or wine
and the liquid drunk - they are said to prolong
life, strengthen the body, nourish tissues, improve
the complexion, etc. They also are said to help in
attunement with God. The Hindus believed that only
diamonds of high quality should be used for therapeutic purposes, for those of inferior quality
might not only fail to cure but might even cause
other illnesses. The diamond is reputed to have
the power to drive away troublesome dreams and un-
reasoning fears, to protect one from injury by ene-
mies and to maintain unity and love. The last mentioned probably influenced its popularity in en-
gagement and wedding rings.

The diamond is a gemstone of the First Ray.

The diamond has a number of interesting physical properties which may contribute to its healing properties. It is very hard, yet it is brittle. In addition, it is fluorescent, phosphores-
cent and triboelectric (gaining a positive charge

by friction). Also, there are two types of diamonds (Types I a & b, II a & b) which differ in transmission in the near ultraviolet and in impurity content. The Type I diamonds contain nitrogen, while the Type II contain aluminum, and very little if any nitrogen. Most diamonds are Type I a.

Feldspar
(Moonstone)

Composition: $(K,Na) AlSi_3O_8$

Crystallography: Triclinic

Form: Usually short prismatic to tabular.

Hardness: 6

Density: 2.56

Cleavage and Fracture: Two cleavages: one perfect, the other moderate.

Color: Colorless, white, pale yellow, grey - with white or blue sheen (adularescence). The sheen is produced by one feldspar being contained within another as a result of unmixing during cooling. Usually orthoclase is the matrix with enclosed albite.

Occurrence: Orthoclase and albite are found in acid igneous rocks, pegmatites and gneisses.

Healing Properties: In one reading Edgar Cayce suggested wearing the moonstone to give one strength and to keep that which is nearest to one closer. The gemstone would be part of one's mental and spiritual consciousness. In another reading, he recommended it to bring out the colors and vibrations to which the entity was sensitive.

Richardson/Huett state that the moonstone incorporates a person's being and feelings, and acts in part as a reflection of the wearer. It is negative for those who have a negative nature and positive for those of a positive nature. It is excellent for psychometry and also for gathering the inner self.

In India, it was believed to bring good fortune and was regarded as a sacred stone.

Moonstone has been closely associated with the moon and its "powers" and thought to be influenced by its phases. The color is similar to that of moonlight, which probably led to its name and some of its uses. The stone was believed to absorb and generate some of the healing properties of the moon, and was employed when the moon was full or approaching full so as to use the stone at its highest powers, and when the moon was at the apex of its powers.

It has been considered a symbol of hope, and talismans were often worn to lift the spirit and strengthen the aura. It was sometimes used as a talisman to aid in treating dropsy and circulatory problems. It has also been worn for protection while travelling. It was thought to act as a guardian, protector and stimulator of the mind, and to keep the mind clear when worn continuously.

The moonstone is used almost always as a stone rather than as a powder. It has also been used by farmers to help promote growth of plants and trees.

Garnet

Composition: $R_3^{2+}R_2^{3+}Si_3O_{12}$

There are two garnet groups: the pyralspites (pyrope, almandine, spessartine), and ugrandites (uvarovite, grossular, andradite). In the pyralspites, R^{2+} is Mg, and R^{3+} is Al, Fe, Mn; while in the ugrandites, R^{2+} is Ca and R^{3+} is Cr, Al, Fe. Substitution within each group can be unlimited, but is very small between the two groups.

Crystallography: Cubic

Form: The form depends in part upon the composition. The ugrandites tend to form dodeca-hedra and the pyralspites form icositetrahedra.

Hardness: 5.5 - 7.5

Density: 3.71 - 4.32

Cleavage and Fracture: One parting

Dispersion: Moderate to high

Color: Colorless, white, grey, yellow, yellowish-green, green, brown, pink, red, black, orange, orange-red, violet-red. The most common gem garnet is the red almandine. The green tsavo-rites are of much greater monetary value, but are rare (especially in stones above 2 carats). Deman-toid, a green andradite, is also a gem garnet.

Occurrence: Garnets are the product of magmatic activity, and of both contact and regional metamorphosis. They are also found in pegmatites.

Healing Properties: Garnets used for

healing were usually almandine and pyrope, the red
and purple-red transparent minerals. They were
thought to counter melancholy and act as a heart
stimulant. In ancient times, there were some who
believed that gazing at a red garnet could lead to
passion, anger and even apoplexy. It is a gemstone of the Sixth Ray.

According to Richardson/Huett, the garnet
is a stone of depth, wonder and purity. It acts
beneficially on the pituitary gland, and also has
the ability to enable a person to reach back into
past lives to gain information useful to the entity in this incarnation. It can be used for protection from outside influences when worn over the
third eye. It has properties useful for giving in-
spiration during times of contemplation. Physically, it is useful in cleansing, purifying and enhancing the forces of the body, and is held over
the spleen for best effect. The green garnet is a
thought purifier and therefore best used in thought
projection, which also then enables it to be used
for healing others. The red garnet is a stone of
profound love. Its energies are those of balance,
peace and solitude; it is a stone of patience and
persistence.

While the red garnets have historically been
used for therapeutic purposes, it is possible that
some of the more recently discovered varieties,
such as the deep emerald-green tsavorites (which
contain traces of vanadium), may have properties
similar to other deep green gemstones such as the
emerald. The green demantoid (which contains small
amounts of chromium) may also have such properties.

The garnet has the highest crystallographic
symmetry of all the gemstones and is a strong crystal former. It will often grow well-developed
crystals and deform those of other compositions
around it. Yet, it is a lesser healing gemstone.
Perhaps it keeps some of its power locked up within itself. The rare-earth garnets, which are most-

known as synthetic crystals, are used in solid-state lasers.

Gold

Composition: Au

Crystallography: Cubic

Form: Dendritic, leafy, filiform or spongy. It also occurs massive, in rough, rounded or flattened grains or scales. Crystals are rare, and are octahedral, dodecahedral or cubic.

Hardness: 2.5 - 3

Density: 19.3

Color: Gold in various shades depending upon impurity content.

Occurrence: Native gold is an igneous mineral related to acidic magmas. It is a late-stage mineral concentrated in post-magmatic solutions and deposited during the various phases of the hydrothermal process. It often combines with tellurium to form gold tellurides, and may also be found dispersed as native gold in sulphide minerals. Gold deposits are also found in placers where they derive from the weathering of primary igneous rocks which removes soluble material while selecting and concentrating the gold by chemical and mechanical means. The famous Witwatersrand deposit consists of gold-bearing conglomerates that have been subjected to late-stage hydrothermal activity depositing gold, and then regionally metamorphosed.

Healing Properties: Edgar Cayce recommended that gold mainly be utilized in chloride solutions both externally in a solution jar to be used with

the "radioactive" (electrical impedence) device,
and internally. In one reading he mentioned gold
as a strengthening influence when worn on the body.
He recommended against using gold as fillings for
carious teeth. Paul Solomon recommended wearing
gold, usually as a setting for a gemstone, to be used in combination for synergistic effects. He felt
it would help stabilize the nerves, and bring warmth
and strength. Tracy Johnson's suggestions include:
to stimulate the heart and thyroid centers to bring
about greater love within the self in order to bring
about harmony between love and will; as a devotional
reminder; as a positive influence on attunement; as
a quieting and healing influence. She did not mention it as a setting for stones, but rather to be
worn alone for itself.

Lama Sing has remarked that while gold can
be very heightening, it tends to slow or retard frequency or vibrations for most people. It can have
beneficial medical effects in minimizing blood poisoning, and in cases where there is difficulty with
the structure of the blood vessels. Gold tends "to
vibrate in terms of the base level of the body's
construction". It significantly affects the first
and second endocrine positions (chakras); it sometimes can cause imbalance in the third center. If
gold is used as a setting for a stone, then it can
be improved to balance between the upper and lower
three endocrinal centers. Gold relates strongly to
the material or physical plane; it is a very earthy
mineral. Therefore, when it is worn in dental work
or as a body adornment, a person may be bombarded
with thoughts or influences from unknown sources.
Gold has a very broad receiving point and may be
symbolically related to God, the all-encompassing
supreme being.

In discussing gold, Richardson/Huett mention that metals have a porous quality that causes
vibrations to come to them; they attract rather
than emit vibrations. Gold is therefore used exten-
sively as a setting for gemstones as it provides a

steadying influence for the stones. It can act as a balancing agent by drawing negative forces from the person while simultaneously retaining the positive forces of the stone. The purer the gold, the more sensitive it is.

Gold has been used for religious objects for thousands of years. It also has been used for treating a number of illnesses, including leprosy, measles, melancholy, lupus, epilepsy, rheumatism, heart disease, sexual dysfunction, locomotor ataxia, and as a chloride in fractional doses for improving digestion and stimulating the brain. It has been thought to impart wisdom and logic.

Gold has been of prime importance throughout the history of man and has an almost magical allure. The color and lustre of gold may have caused people in ancient times to assume a relation between gold and the sun - and therefore to a deity or prime source. It has an allure beyond its intrinsic value or physical utility.

Some recommend bathing in the sea while wearing gold to enhance its effects by a chemical reaction which produces a more soluble gold chloride (which is better absorbed by the skin).

Hematite

Composition: Fe_2O_3

Crystallography: Trigonal

Form: Usually massive, but may be found as crystals with rhombohedral or pinacoidal faces. It is often granular, reniform, stalactitic or oölitic.

Hardness: 5 - 6.5

Density: 5.26

Cleavage and Fracture: No cleavage; two partings.

Color: Steel grey to black with metallic or sub-metallic lustre; red, brownish-red.

Occurrence: Hematite is often a product of regional or contact metamorphism. It also occurs in hydrothermal concentrations and as a product of weathering or precipitation in large bodies of water.

Healing Properties: Tracy Johnson suggested wearing hematite in a ring on the right hand to focus energy patterns and emotions for better balance between the mental, physical and spiritual. In ancient Egypt it was used to check hemorrhages, to reduce inflammation, and to treat hysteria. It was thought that hematite would have a negative physical effect if worn too long.

Hematite may have had importance to the Pueblo Indians, as there are indications that it was worn with turquoise as an amulet.

Jade
A. Jadeite

Composition: $NaAlSi_2O_6$

Crystallography: Monoclinic

Form: Usually found in granular aggregates with tough, interlocking crystals.

Hardness: 6.5 - 7

Density: 3.33

Cleavage and Fracture: No cleavage.

Color: Light green to white, colorless, green, yellow-green, yellow-brown, black, orange, red, violet.

Occurrence: Jadeite is generally found in metamorphosed alkaline rocks (usually serpentine).

B. Nephrite

Composition: $Ca_2(Mg,Fe)_5Si_8O_{22}(OH)_2$

Crystallography: Monoclinic

Form: Usually found in densely packed radiating or fibrous aggregates; also as long prismatic crystals without terminal faces.

Hardness: 5.5 - 6

Density: 2.9 - 3.3

Cleavage and Fracture: No cleavage

Color: Creamy-beige (mutton fat jade), green, yellowish, greyish-brown, yellow-green, and black. The nephrite colors are not as varied or as intense as those of jadeite, and tend to be dark and somber.

Occurrence: Nephrite is a metasomatic product in calcareous rocks and in serpentinites.

*

Healing Properties: Jadeite and nephrite are both termed jade, and no distinction has been made as to therapeutic properties.

In one reading, Cayce suggested that wearing jade in combination with pearls would create positive vibrations to facilitate emotional expression. Solomon recommended keeping a piece of jade in the pocket or on the person to be rubbed in meditation or when attempting to attune to the needs of others.

Richardson/Huett state that jade can be simultaneously piercing and tranquil. It reaches the depth of wisdom within a person and to the depth of a problem; it also can bring the peace that is necessary to a particular problem. It is a good stone for meditation. The various colors have an effect upon the therapeutic qualities of the stones, and when used for healing (particularly emotional healing) one should first select a suitable color and then place this stone on the necessary body area or chakra. Jade strongly influences the heart center and also, by acting as a magnet, it draws impurities from the glands, thus cleansing them. Red jade can bring forth emotional problems (such as anger) so that they can be better defined and therefore resolved. Orange is a stimulating color, helping the wearer to determine the causes of lack of energy and to reverse the condition. Yellow jade works mainly on the solar plexus and also stimulates the flow of bile to aid in digestion and eliminations. This color should not be worn directly on the body, but rather in a purse or outer garment. The blue jade has a mental rather than physical effect, and is the most peaceful of the colors. Green jade also has a beneficial effect upon the emotions. Salmon stimulates the adrenal glands, lavender radiates love, beauty and security and also is beneficial for healing mental problems.

Jade has been used to protect against a number of illnesses, including urinary tract problems, digestive complaints, eye problems, and "earthy ailments". Amulets of jade have been worn for safe travel, and in ancient Egypt it was used in burials and was believed to have mystical powers. This stone has been of importance in a number of civilizations. The Chinese believed that it provided a link between the spiritual and the worldly, and Confucius said that it served as a reminder of the integrity of mind and soul. The Chinese regarded jade as a musical gem, and made chimes out of a series of oblong pieces. The sounds were said to have beneficial emotional effects. Jade has often been used for carving objects, most of which have significance in themselves, so it sometimes has been the combination of the object and the jade. Jade talismans have been thought to confer long life and an easy and peaceful passing from this plane. To the Aztecs, green was a color of loyalty.

Jade is a gemstone of the Third Ray.

Jet

Composition: C + impurities

Crystallography: Amorphous

Form: Massive

Hardness: 2.4 - 4

Density: 1.30 - 1.35

Cleavage and Fracture: Fracture conchoidal. Brittle.

Color: Black, brownish

Occurrence: Jet is fossilized wood called lignite which is a form of brown coal.

Healing Properties: At one time, jet was used in powdered form and mixed with beeswax as an ointment to treat tumors. The powder also was mixed with wine or water and used for toothaches, either as a powder or drunk. The powder was sometimes burned to produce fumes which were then used to repel germs of plague, pestilence and fever, and also as a fumigent. The fumes were also used to treat epilepsy, to quiet hallucinations from fever, to combat hysteria, and to treat dropsy, diseases of the stomach, neck swellings and headaches.

Solid pieces of jet, usually in the form of amulets, were used to dispel depression and fearful thoughts, and to protect from the effects of thunderstorms.

Lazurite
(Lapis Lazuli)

Composition: $(Na, Ca)_8 (AlSiO_4)_6 (SO_4, Cl, S)_2$

Lazurite is a member of the sodalite group of minerals. Other members are:

Sodalite $Na_8 (AlSiO_4)_6 Cl_2$

Nosean $Na_8 (AlSiO_4)_6 SO_4$

Haüyne $Na_6 Ca_2 (AlSiO_4)_6 SO_4$

Crystallography: Tetragonal

Form: Often forms rhombododecahedra; usually granular or in compact masses.

Hardness: 5.5 - 6

Density: 2.14 - 2.45

Cleavage and Fracture: One indistinct cleavage.

Colors: Blue to bluish-green, often mixed with other minerals such as calcite, pyrite, sometimes forming a variegated stone; also grey, yellowish red or purple.

Occurrence: Minerals which have been called Lapis Lazuli are often not pure lazurite, and sometimes are not lazurite at all. The members of the sodalite group closely resemble one another, and usually occur inter-mixed with each other. Sodalite, nosean and haüyne are found in volcanic alkali rocks; sodalite also occurs in alkali plutonic rocks and related pegmatites. Lazurite generally occurs as a result of the effects of contact meta-

somatism by alkali plutonic magma in limestone.
While lazurite has a somewhat different geologic
origin from the other minerals in this group, it is
probable that the other members have been identified
as lazurite in the past. Also, lazurite can occur
admixed with other sodalites, and sometimes does.
Years ago, minerals were identified predominantly
by physical appearance and hardness. Small differences in chemical composition probably were not considered, as analytical methods were crude.

Healing properties: According to Edgar
Cayce, lapis lazuli brings strength to the body and
makes the body more sensitive to higher vibrations.
In one reading he claimed that it "is itself an em-
anation of vibrations of the elements that give vitality, virility, strength, and that of assurance
in self". (Reading #1981-1). He often cautioned
the wearer to encase the mineral in thin glass as
the vibrations are very strong. He also mentioned
using rough (unpolished) minerals for greater effect. There is an unresolved problem in the Cayce
material, however, as he often referred to lapis
lazuli as a copper-bearing sedimentary mineral,
which it is not, and some confusion exists as to
the identity of the mineral he called lapis lazuli.
Carley believes that it may be chrysocolla and/or
azurite. Azurite seems the more probable mineral
from its physical appearance, although there was
one reference to a blue-green chalcedony containing
impurities such as copper or iron, giving it that
color. Azurite is a soft mineral, and the readings
mention a soft mineral. The hardness of chrysocolla varies from 2 to 7 Mohs, depending upon silica
content. There is a silicified form of azurite and
malachite which is translucent in thin sections.
This, rather than chrysocolla, may have been the
blue-green chalcedony. Also, chrysocolla has not
been referred to as a healing mineral by others or
in folklore. The confusion about identity also cre-
ates problems as to the therapeutic properties of

lapis lazuli as seen by this great psychic. He may
have been referring to both azurite and lazurite;
it is possible that they once had the same name as
they had not as yet been properly identified. This
is an unresolved area.

Other psychics and also folklore attribute
healing properties to lapis lazuli. According to
folklore, it can be used to treat eye troubles.
According to Solomon, it can assist in the development of creative mental images for the purpose of
telepathic communication, especially of inner
planes, when taped over the third eye area of the
forehead. He felt that lapis lazuli was a useful
stone for attunement and spiritual purification.
The effects of this mineral are more spiritual than
physical, while those of azurite would be more on
the physical plane. According to the doctrine of
Seven Rays of Life, it is a stone of the Second Ray,
as is sodalite. In ancient times, powdered lapis
lazuli was used as an external dressing for boils
and ulcerations, and internally as a purge and also
for melancholy.

Richardson/Huett state that lapis lazuli
has the property of enabling the wearer to tune his
/her etheric body to the vibrations of the particular stone, which has the effect of facilitating the
opening of many of the chakras. They caution that
one should do this only with the highest of inten-
tions. It has a fine energy vibration towards
which one has to reach, as it does not come to the
person. It affects the Kundalini and heart centers,
and is very useful in helping to discover the gold-
en qualities of another person. They believe that
lapis lazuli is best worn above the diaphragm to
draw energy to the higher spiritual centers. It
does not so much give power as it tends to bring
forth that which is already contained within the
person.

Kunz has suggested that the original mineral used for healing the eyes was a copper oxide

called lapis armenus, and that lazurite was later
substituted for it because of the greater intrinsic
value of the lazurite. The identity of lapis armenus is not known but may have been azurite, which is
blue in powdered form as well as in crystal (while
chrysocolla and a number of copper oxides or phos-
phate minerals have whitish powders). It may be
that lapis armenus was the mineral Cayce referred
to.

In some civilizations, lapis lazuli is tied
up with sex symbolism. There are references in As-
syrian texts to symbolic sex organs being carved of
this material. The Egyptian Sun symbol also was often carved of lapis lazuli.

Lapis lazuli had considerable religious significance in ancient times. It was probably one of
the stones of the high-priest's breastplate. It is
reported that Moses inscribed the ten commandments
on blocks of this mineral. Centuries ago, it was
used as an offering to the Lord of the Universe by
the priest-kings in ceremonies in the Temple of
Heaven. In ancient Egypt it was the stone used for
the image of truth worn by the chief-justice. The
high-priest is said to have worn an amulet of the
Goddess of Truth (Mat) around his neck. There are
references to it in the "Book of The Dead". It was
carved in the form of an eye and was inscribed with
the 140th chapter of that book. Offerings were made
before this eye on the last day of Mechir, the day
on which the Supreme God Rama was believed to place
such an image on his head. Lapis lazuli is one of
the seven precious stones of Buddhism. In various
societies it has been used in amulets, seals, orna-
ments and scarabs.

It may well be that the healing powers of
this mineral derive from its spiritual connection,
and it would thus be of value in helping to produce
an elevation of consciousness, which may then have
secondary physical effects.

Lapis lazuli is a gemstone of the Second Ray.

Magnetite

Composition: Fe_3O_4

Crystallography: Cubic

Form: Crystals octahedral; sometimes dode-cahedral.

Hardness: 5.5 - 6.5

Density: 5.2

Cleavage and Fracture: One parting

Color: Black

Occurrence: Magnetite can be formed under a variety of geologic conditions such as contact metamorphism, regional metamorphism, igneous intrusives, hydrothermal deposition.

Healing Properties: Magnetite is a gemstone of the First Ray and is a stone of stability. It is a natural magnet and may influence the alignment of the hemoglobin (which contains iron) with the earth's magnetic poles.

In some societies it was once thought to attract love. It also has been thought to help induce healthful sleep.

According to Richardson/Huett, lodestone (magnetite) has the effect of causing the release of the mind from the body by projecting the mind to distant places. Physically, it is effective in treating conditions of the lungs, particularly the lower lobes.

Malachite
(Lapis Ligurius)

Composition: $Cu_2CO_3(OH)_2$

Crystallography: Monoclinic

Form: Malachite is usually found in botryoidal or tuberose aggregates with radial fibrous textures. It is massive and sometimes banded. At times it is stalactitic, and also forms incrustations.

Hardness: 3.5 - 4

Density: 4.05

Cleavage and Fracture: One perfect cleavage. Fracture uneven, brittle.

Color: Green to dark green

Occurrence: Malachite is a sedimentary mineral, a product of the weathering of copper sulphide minerals. It is also an alteration product of azurite.

Healing Properties: According to Edgar Cayce, malachite helps to provide physical protection for the wearer. His readings indicate that the combination of the elements in this mineral, not only the copper, would be beneficial as a protecting influence.

Tracy Johnson has postulated that it can stimulate a more harmonious expression of the (often diverse) qualities of love and will do so when worn about the neck.

Richardson/Huett believe that malachite acts as a mirror, reflecting the inner feelings of a person. They suggest that a person consider his/ her mood before wearing this stone; it is better worn when psychologically "up". It is not of much value for physical healing, and they recommend a- gainst its use for this purpose.

Malachite was used in ancient Egypt to treat cholera and rheumatism and also to protect children from evil spirits. In the middle ages it was used to protect against the "evil eye". In the East, talismans of malachite were often worn to ensure sleep, protect from lightning, and for fidelity in love and friendship.

It has also been used for cosmetic purposes; in prehistoric Egypt, it was ground with galena (PbS) on slate palettes, mixed with water, and then painted on the eyelids.

Malachite is a gemstone of the Third Ray.

Olivine
(Peridot)

Composition: $(Mg,Fe)_2SiO_4$
(Forsterite and Fayalite).

Crystallography: Orthorhombic

Form: Crystals are thick tabular. Usually massive.

Hardness: 6.5 - 7

Density: 3.6 - 4.4

Cleavage and Fracture: Weak to moderate cleavages.

Dispersion: Low to moderate

Color: Forsterite = green, pale lemon yellow. Fayalite = amber brown, brown, olive green.

Occurrence: Olivine is found in basic and ultrabasic igneous rocks and in metamorphosed dolomites.

Healing Properties: Olivine has been used for protection. It has been considered advisable to set the stones in gold to enhance their power.

It has tentatively been allocated as a gemstone of the Third Ray.

Richardson/Huett state that peridot should be used only by persons who are clear minded and therefore able to take a long view of life, as its vibrations are very light. In healing, it is useful mainly to treat the spirit rather than the body, and is of value to those who are spiritually developed. It affects the upper three chakras.

Pearl

Composition: $CaCO_3$ (aragonite).

Aragonite (84-88%) + H_2O (2%) + conchiolin (10-14%)

Crystallography: Orthorhombic

Form: The minute crystals are radially or-
ientated in a concentric structure giving rounded
forms.

Hardness: 2.5 - 4.5

Density: 2.6 - 2.85

Cleavage and Fracture: No cleavage; fracture uneven.

Color: White, cream, rose, black, grey,
bronze, blue, green.

Occurrence: Pearls are usually found in
salt water and the most important are formed within
the shell of an oyster known as Pinctada. They are
also found in conch shells and abalone. There is a
fresh-water animal (the mussel kio) which is found
inhabiting rivers worldwide and which forms pearls.

Cultured pearls are created by the inser-
tion of a bead of mother-of-pearl along with pieces
of tissue from the mantle into the body of the oyster. The oysters thus treated are left for from
three to six years at depths of seven to ten feet
in the ocean, and the layers of nacre accumulate a-
round the bead.

Healing Properties: Cayce recommended that
pearls be worn directly upon the body, touching the

flesh. The vibrations of this gem are healing as well as creative because of the way it is produced - from irritation of the organism which defended itself by secreting self-protecting material around this piece of "grit"; thus beauty was formed by overcoming hardship. The wearing of pearls would help to develop an even temperament as well as aid in healing, in giving strength and developing purity.

Paul Solomon suggests that the wearing of pearls would be beneficial in meditation for some people. Tracy Johnson has indicated that wearing pearls at night would stimulate dreaming.

According to Lama Sing, the pearl relates to people in a different manner from minerals because of its organic origin. The spherical form has a somewhat significant effect upon the lower three endocrinal centers. It affects the abdominal area and also somewhat the adsorption of drosses in the body. The absorption of vibrations from the body can cause pearls to become discolored. Certain groups of peoples have used them to heighten fertility.

Pearls have been held in high esteem throughout history. The ancient Hindus included the pearl as one of the five precious gems in the magical necklace of Vishnu (along with diamond, ruby, emerald and sapphire). It has been held as a symbol of the moon, an object of worship by a number of peoples. The color of the pearl also had an effect: gold for wealth, black for philosophy, pink for beauty, red for health and energy, and grey for thought. It was an emblem of purity, innocence and peace, and was worn by young girls in ancient times to protect their virginity.

According to Swedenborg, pearls represented truth and the knowledge of truth, celestial and spiritual knowledge, faith and charity.

Richardson/Huett state that the pearl has the ability to reach the depth of the personality of an individual. It is a good gem to use for

meditation; it has the effect of focussing the at-
tention and pulling together the mental and spiritual forces. They believe that it has no effect
upon the physical body, although it can be soothing
to the pituitary gland, particularly when the person is under great stress.

As "natural" pearls are rare and very expensive, the question arises whether cultured pearls
would also be effective in healing. Richardson/
Huett believe that their power would be rather low
and therefore of little effect. But, cultured
pearls are in a way a natural product formed by mol-
lusks around pieces of nacre embedded in mantle.
The main difference between cultured and natural
pearls is that in the former, the "irritant" is in-
serted by man and these pearls are cultivated, while
in the latter the "irritant" enters the shell on its
own. There would be slight differences between
them. This writer believes therefore, that cultured
pearls probably would be efficacious, although probably not as much as natural pearls.

At one time, pulverized pearl was stirred
in milk and drunk by an individual to cure irrita-
bility. Pearls have been worn to treat for acid
indigestion, especially with an aversion to fatty
foods. Powdered pearls were sometimes dissolved in
water or wine to treat indigestion, and whole pearls
were also used for this purpose. In the latter
case, they were steeped in water, wine or a medicin-
al liquid, and the fluid was then drunk. It could
be that the effect of the $CaCO_3$ was to neutralize
an acid condition in the stomach. Calcium is also
a soothing substance for nerves, and may have eased
digestive spasms.

In ancient times, in rituals, the priests
wore a gemstone over the "third eye", and a pearl
was probably one of the stones so used, particularly as it was considered to have a large effect on
the mind.

SiO$_2$ Minerals
A. Quartz

Composition: SiO$_2$ (the color of amethyst is due to traces of manganese).

Crystallography: Trigonal

Form: Prismatic, often terminated on one or both ends. Also commonly massive.

Hardness: 7

Density: 2.65

Cleavage and Fracture: Conchoidal fracture; no cleavage.

Color: Clear, colorless, milky, brown, yellowish-brown, blackish, purple to bluish violet, yellow.

Dispersion: Low

Occurrence: Quartz is one of the most abundant minerals in the crust of the earth, and can have an igneous, sedimentary or metamorphic origin. In pegmatites, it often forms large euhedral crystals some of which may weigh up to forty tons. It is deposited from aqueous solutions over a long period of time and this type of slow growth encourages high crystal perfection and large size. Quartz deposited from hydrothermal solutions is usually clear or amethyst and assumes the form of long prisms. These crystals tend to be of small to moderate size.

Healing Properties:

AMETHYST Cayce suggested that wearing amethyst
would help to control the temperament, facilitate
healing and give strength during periods of great
activity. It can be worn as amulets or as jewelry.
Solomon recommends amethyst for increasing spiritual attunement. In one reading he mentioned that
it would settle rather than lengthen vibrations; in
another that it would be beneficial in a feeling of
purification, warmth and healing. Johnson also indicates that amethyst aids in raising ideals and uplifting the spirit. Lama Sing refers to it as a
purifier. He also indicates some kind of relationship between amethyst and beryl, referring to beryl
as a form of amethyst and suggests that they are
useful in balancing and can heighten the personality to the good nature of the individual. They may
be useful to those who are depressed or under emotional stress.

Richardson/Huett believe that the amethyst
is a powerful stone which can greatly benefit a
person both physically and spiritually. The ability of this mineral to absorb forces which are being directed to a person allows it to repel the vibrations which the person does not need, and which
therefore are not right for him. The amethyst can
purify and amplify healing rays; the color itself
is one of purification. This stone works directly
on the blood vessels and purifies the blood, and
it is of value in treating blood clots as well as
in drawing out impurities. The stone should be
moved about the body and placed in the area of the
physical problem. It also has an effect upon the
lungs. They suggest breathing in deeply the color
of the stone while meditating totally on the color.
This will help with problems of asthma and respiratory allergies. Amethyst can also be used for re-
charging energy within the etheric body by placing
the stone over the head while out of doors and let-
ting the sunlight focus through it to the crown

chakra. When healing others, wear it over the
third eye center. It is best worn over the heart
center for general purposes. They state that amethyst has the ability to alter molecular structures
by causing an inner struggle which then raises the
vibrational rate, and causes the atoms to rearrange
themselves into a purer form.

Other therapeutic properties ascribed to
amethyst include protection from evil influences,
clearing the mind, an antidote to drunkenness, ex-
pelling poisons, facilitating attunements, aiding
in circulatory disorders, conferring "second sight"
by opening the psychic centers, a soothing and calm-
ing influence, treating gout, insomnia and nervous
headache, and to induce pleasant dreams.

Amethyst may have been the ninth stone of
the High Priest's breastplate. It has had religious significance for centuries and is used even today as the stone in the ring worn by Catholic Bishops. The Rosicrucians believe it to be a symbol of
the divine male sacrifice.

Amethyst is a gemstone of the Seventh Ray.

ROCK CRYSTAL Rock Crystal has been used in Scot-
land for general healing. The patient drank water
in which it had been placed. It possesses qualities stimulating to clairvoyance and provides
"clear sleep", and is the choice material for crystal gazing. In Japan it is a symbol of the purity
of the infinity of space and also of patience and
perseverance. It is one of the seven precious
stones of Buddhism; in the Tibetan system the Eas-
tern region of heaven is constructed of white crystal.

Richardson/Huett state that rock crystal
works especially with the third eye, and has the
effect of causing a person to reach a place (infinity) where he/she has clear vision. Thus it is
useful for crystal balls, as it enables the mind to
project itself and become one with everything.
When used in healing, it has the property of ampli-

fying the energies of the person using the stone,
and it can change to accommodate each person. It
is useful in treating most illnesses, and a pyramid-
shaped crystal is recommended for this purpose.
The pointed end is to be held against the palm with
the flat side facing outwards.

Rock crystal is a gemstone of the First Ray.

CITRINE   This yellow mineral has sometimes been
misidentified as topaz. It is softer than topaz,
and has a lower dispersion. The yellow crystal is
said to have the power to draw color.

It is a gemstone of the Fifth Ray.

Quartz has certain physical and chemical properties which may be factors in its therapeutic effects. Its structure is non-centro-symmetric and
it possesses the properties of piezo-electricity
(developing a charge from heat). The first-mention-
ed property enables quartz crystals to be used in a
number of electronic devices such as radio, radar,
instruments of communication, clocks and watches.
The atoms within the structure are arranged in a
helix or spiral which may be either right or left-
handed in twist. As living matter has a left hand
turn in the cellular matter, perhaps the direction
of twist of the quartz plays a role in its effectiveness. It may be that only those stones that rotate to the left are effective, or that they are effective for certain purposes and those which rotate
to the right are for other purposes.

Janet and Colin Bord speculate that the
special healing properties of members of the quartz
family may derive from their ability to retain an
electrical charge. The charge may have come from
currents within the earth or from those of a healer
(either acting as a conductor for Universal forces
or containing healing energies within him/her self).

B. Chalcedony

Composition: SiO_2 (+ trace H_2O)

Crystallography: Trigonal (a fibrous cryptocrystalline quartz with some admixed water or opal).

Form: Massive

Hardness: 6 - 7

Density: 2.58

Cleavage and fracture: No cleavage; fracture conchoidal.

Color: A variety of colors from white to black. Some colors are given specific names. Heliotrope or bloodstone is green with red spots; carnelian is clear red; prase is translucent green; onyx is banded with black and white layers; sardonyx is banded with red and white layers; agate is a variegated chalcedony and quartz mixture; jasper is an impure opaque quartz. The color depends upon mineral impurities including oxides of Fe, Mn, Ti, Cr, Ni.

Occurrence: Chalcedonies are of sedimentary origin which form either as gelatinous masses that slowly dehydrate and crystallize, or by deposition from slowly moving ground water which deposits silica over a long period of time. The banded chalcedonies are produced in the latter manner; they also occur as deposits in pockets in volcanic rock.

Healing Properties:
AGATE According to Edgar Cayce agate is useful to help awaken and open the inner self for receptivity and to supply strength during times of great activity. Paul Solomon believed it to be a stabilizing and grounding influence. Other therapeutic properties attributed to agate include driving away bad dreams, a charm against scorpions and spiders, a

talisman for athletes, banishing fear, giving protection from storms, hardening the tender gums of children, protecting children from falling, protecting vision, vanquishing all earthly obstacles, and guarding from dangers.

Richardson/Huett state that agate is beneficial to the stomach, particularly when it feels upset. It is not useful for emotional or mental stomach upsets, however. It helps with gaining a feeling of acceptance and a realization that "this too shall pass". It has the ability to simultaneously tap several chakras, causing them to work together. It is a fairly complete but subtle stone which can bring about a reversal of energy flow within the body or the center that is upset.

To Swedenborg it was a symbol of the spiritual love of good. Agate is believed to have been the eighth stone in the breastplate of the High Priest. It has been used widely in amulets and talismans, carved seals, signets and finger rings.

Agate is a gemstone of the Fourth Ray.

BLOODSTONE (heliotrope): Edgar Cayce indicated that bloodstone was a healing stone, in good part because of its color. It brings more harmony in vibrations and may help in making decisions. It has also been used to staunch hemorrhages and prevent nosebleeds.

Richardson/Huett state that bloodstone affects the Kundalini center, and, to be effective, should only be used by one who has already aroused this center. It should be used unset, and moved along the spine of the person. It can be a powerful stone in the hands of a master; it stimulates energy to move upwards from the base of the spine, and aids in the alignment of the centers, and of the etheric and spiritual bodies as well. Its vibrations, which are slow, are not of a physical nature.

CARNELIAN Carnelian has been thought to staunch

hemorrhages, prevent nosebleeds, and purify blood.
It was used by early Egyptians for a number of amulets. It is one of the seven precious substances
of Buddhism, and is highly venerated among Lamaists.
In the East, it was thought to protect from the en-
vy of others and to protect from evil. The prophet
Mohammed wore a silver ring set with an engraved
carnelian and used as a seal. It is a gemstone of
the Sixth Ray.

According to Richardson/Huett, carnelian is
useful to give a push by stimulating interest to
someone who is lethargic. Physically, it can help
stimulate the liver, and aid in the self-purifica-
tion of this vital organ.

JASPER   In ancient times, jasper was used to cure
queasy stomachs and soothe the nerves. It was commonly used for amulets, seals, and scarabs. Jasper
is the chief stone of the Fourth Ray.

Richardson/Huett state that jasper is a subtle rather than a strong stone which works over a
long period of time. It is of greatest value in
healing when worn just below the throat chakra
where it has the effect of changing the vibrations
from the lower parts of the body as they move upward into the head. Drinking water in which a
green jasper has been immersed for two to three
days is also recommended to prepare the body to receive other helpful vibrations. When worn with an
opal, it can have a moderating yet complementary
effect upon the power of the opal.

ONYX   Richardson/Huett suggest that onyx is an excellent stone to use in psychometry as it has the
ability to transmute the vibrations of another person. It does not draw negative forces to itself,
but mainly tells about the person wearing it. In
healing, it tends to give physical strength and
emotional stability in times of high stress, in
part by preventing the draining of energy from the
body. It is particularly helpful in stabilizing

the area of the solar plexus, and should be worn near the heart center for this use. Pearls and dia- monds have a complementary effect on onyx and, when worn as pairs, enhance each others' power.

SARDONYX   In a reading, sardonyx was mentioned by Cayce as a stone to be carried on the person in sta- tuettes, pins, buttons or pieces. He felt it was not a protective stone, but had a vibratory force which would influence choices. Others have sugges- ted that it encourages happiness and good fortune, and banishes grief. According to Swedenborg it rep- resents the love of good and light.

According to Richardson/Huett, it is a very physical stone, better used by those of an aggres- sive nature. It has an effect upon the bone marrow and can help alleviate cell disturbances of the mar- row.

C. Opal

Composition: $SiO_2 \cdot 2H_2O$ (H_2O = 1 - 21%, usually in precious opal).

Crystallography: Amorphous (composed of an aggregate of tiny spherical particles and is a sol- idified gel).

Form: Hardened gel

Hardness: 5.5 - 6.5

Density: 1.99 - 2.25

Cleavage and Fracture: No cleavage; frac- ture conchoidal, brittle.

Dispersion: Very low

Color: Colorless, white, yellow, orange, red, yellowish-brown, green, blue, grey, black, violet.

Occurrence: Opal is formed by the action

of water dissolving silica from minerals and rede-
positing it. It is also deposited around geysers.

Healing Properties: Cayce has suggested
that wearing opals would be beneficial in attunement, a centering influence for the self and others
and an aid to spiritual purification to be a chan-
nel for teaching truths to others. The correct attitude is important in the wearer. Paul Solomon
and Tracy Johnson believe it is a powerful healing
influence which may be too strong for some people
- those who are not as yet willing to act as chan-
nels for healing energies. Solomon mentions that
gazing into its depths would bring meditative
thoughts that would be peaceful and uplifting as
reminders of purity. According to Lama Sing, the
opal is a significant gem which affects largely the
spiritual-mental link. When worn upon a head garment, it has an effect on the pineal-pituitary centers by amplifying or clarifying levels of vibration by intensifying or purifying segments. They
can act as tuners. It affects the awareness of the
past, present and future. It is powerful in terms
of psychic development.

Richardson/Huett state that the opal has
the effect of amplifying a person's traits and
therefore should be worn only by those who are
well-centered and mature. It has the ability to
focus upon the need of a person and also to focus
on the root of problems.

In ancient times, the opal was thought to
be a very powerful healing stone, and was believed
to open up the senses of the third eye. It was
thought to favor children, the theatre, amusements,
friendships and feelings, and to enhance memory and
lend clarity to the mind, and to strengthen the
eyesight. It was at one time a stone of love which
would reverse its effect and become unlucky to
faithless lovers. It can entice one away from ev-
eryday affairs to the ideal world of high purpose
and far horizons. This may be a factor in the opal

being considered unlucky; it has a negative effect
on those who are not prepared to sacrifice the personal for an ideal. It can be a protective stone
providing justice, harmony, protection and emotional depth.

The great power ascribed to the opal may be
due to the water content. Water is a polar mole-
cule (it has a positive and a negative pole, + -)
and it is possible that there is a lining-up of
these molecules with the fluids or fields of the
body, thus enhancing its effect.

The qualities ascribed to the opal are predominantly mystical, and in ancient times it was
rarely used for physical healing, except for the
eyes. It was believed to be very sensitive to the
atmosphere around it, symbolizing the immediate
prospects and hopes of its owner by the degree of
its brightness.

Silver

Composition: Ag

Crystallography: Cubic

Form: Crystals are rare, usually cubic, octahedral or dodecahedral. It is commonly found in arborescent and wiry forms. It is also massive, scaly, leafy, porous and thin plates.

Hardness: 2.5 - 3

Density: 10.5

Color: Silver polishes to a brilliant white and possesses the greatest reflectivity of any natural substance. At normal temperatures, pure silver is the best known conductor of electricity.

Occurrence: Silver most frequently forms as a hydrothermal product; it also occurs as a product of weathering under reducing conditions of silver-bearing minerals.

Healing Properties: Cayce mentioned, in passing, that silver has a stabilizing influence. Solomon recommended using silver as a setting for certain gemstones (turquoise, yellow and purple stones). It seems to enhance the stone. Johnson suggested wearing intricate, hand-made objects of silver, either alone or as a setting for a blue stone, to help those of quiet attitudes and natures. She further mentions silver as being useful for cleansing through the pores of the skin.

Lama Sing has mentioned that silver has its primary influence on the second to third endocrinal centers, and also has a lesser effect upon the sixth. It affects the throat and heart centers by its influence on blood flow. The wearing of silver has been thought to improve the voice quality of those who do much public speaking.

Richardson/Huett suggest that silver attracts the physical (or lesser) vibrations to itself. It is of strong character, although not particularly materialistic.

Other properties ascribed to silver include repressing and relieving epilepsy and allied nervous seizures, protection against neuralgic attacks, aid in healing sores, preserving the hair and fortifying the bronchial membranes and the throat.

There are claims that the therapeutic properties of silver are enhanced while bathing in the sea, as chlorides of silver are then formed and these are more soluble and therefore better absorbed by the skin.

Spinel

Composition: $R^{2+} R^{3+} O_4$; where R^{2+} can be Mg, Zn, Fe, Mn; and R^{3+} can be Al, (Al,Cr), Fe.

Crystallography: Cubic

Form: Crystals are usually octahedral, sometimes modified by the cube or dodecahedron.

Hardness: 5.5 - 8

Density: 3.58 - 3.98

Cleavage and Fracture: One indistinct parting. Fracture conchoidal. Brittle.

Dispersion: Low to moderate.

Color: Red, blue, green, brown, black, grey, lilac, purple, orange, orange-red, rose-red, almost colorless.

Occurrence: Spinels are high-temperature minerals and form in basic igneous rocks, in highly aluminous metamorphic rocks, and in contact metasomatic limestones.

Healing Properties: Richardson/Huett believe that spinel has the ability to renew energy and vitality on a short term basis. They state that it brings the solar plexus and will centers into alignment, thus bringing about an opening of these centers, and should therefore be worn on the chest.

Spinels themselves have not had therapeutic properties attributed to them elsewhere, but they have often been mistakenly identified as a more valuable gemstone (the most common error being with the deep red spinel - called Balas ruby - which has often been misidentified as ruby). It is possible, therefore, that spinels have been inadvertently used in healing, although the results would be unknown. Perhaps the deep red spinel has properties similar to ruby, but at a lower intensity, or it may be similar to garnet.

Topaz

Composition: $Al_2SiO_4(F, OH)_2$

Crystallography: Orthorhombic

Form: It usually occurs as short, prismatic crystals showing a number of forms. Crystals of topaz may reach weights of hundreds of pounds, and gemstones of up to 20,000 carats have been cut from them.

Hardness: 8

Density: 3.52 - 3.57

Cleavage and Fracture: One perfect cleavage.

Color: The most desirable colors are pink and deep orange. Other colors are white, colorless, grey, blue, green, yellow, yellow-brown, tan, beige and red.

Dispersion: Low

Occurrence: Topaz is an igneous mineral which is usually formed in pegmatites and high-temperature quartz veins. It also occurs in cavities in granite and rhyolite as a late-stage mineral, and in contact metamorphic zones. It may become concentrated in placers.

Healing Properties: Cayce felt that it was a source of strength through the action of its color, beauty and clarity. The yellow tint has a beneficial vibrational effect on those who are especially influenced by the planets Mercury, Venus and

Mars. Solomon and Johnson also have referred to topaz as a source of strength, and they attribute much of its properties to its color. To Solomon, it gave greater strength for health; while Johnson felt that its effects were more of a mental nature (strengthening purpose in the mind and helping to bring out individuality).

According to Richardson/Huett, topaz is useful in treating tension headaches as it helps bring about relaxation of the cells within the head. It is therefore also useful for insomnia and exogenous depression, as it can absorb and disperse or dissolve lesser vibrations. It is a generally beneficial stone because of this ability to draw off negativity and impart lightness, joy and love.

Other powers attributed to topaz include banishing night terrors and fear of death, assisting fidelity in friendship, protection during epidemics, soothing of wild passions, strengthening of the teeth and bones, allaying anger and grief, preventing hemorrhages, diminishing madness, increasing wisdom, giving a glimpse of the beyond, securing a painless passing from this life to the next, guarding against untimely death, healing through trust, and treating disorders of kidneys, liver, and respiratory system.

Topaz also had religious significance in ancient Egypt, where it was the symbol of the Sun God, Ra, the giver of life and fertility. In the East it is reputed to have mystical and magical powers, and some mediums believed it aided in contacting astral beings. It has sacred associations for the Burmese and is one of the gems set in the Nan-Ratan, a piece of jewelry which is the most important part of the Regalia of Burma.

Topaz is a gemstone of the Fifth Ray.

Tourmaline

Composition:

$(Na,Ca)(Mg,Fe,Li)_3Al_6B_3Si_6O_{27}(OH)_4$

Crystallography: Trigonal

Form: Prismatic to acicular, crystals often striated. Also in radiating aggregates or dendrites. When prismatic crystals have well-formed faces, they are found on only one end of the prism, the end which has a positive charge when the crystal is heated.

Hardness: 7 - 7.5

Density: 2.9 - 3.7

Cleavage and Fracture: Two poor cleavages.

Dispersion: Weak to moderate

Color: All colors are found, from colorless to black. Crystals are often zoned by color either along their length or concentrically. The green shades are caused by either V or Cr substituting for Al.

Occurrence: Tourmaline is the product of hydrothermal and pegmatitic deposits under the action of boron. It is found in crystalline schists, granites, and pegmatites, gneiss, marble and contact metamorphic rocks. Its chemistry has been described by John Ruskin as being "more like a medieval doctor's prescription than the making of a reputable mineral".

Healing Properties: Tracy Johnson has suggested that tourmaline could be useful for main-

taining a balance in relationships with others for
those who work with others in a compassionate and
healing way. It has also been used to calm, dispel
fear and induce tranquil sleep. The predominant
healing colors appear to be green and pink. The
green is thought to attract success and the pink to
attract love and friendship. These two colors are
often found together in one zoned crystal.

Richardson/Huett believe that tourmaline
has its greatest effect on the intestinal tract and
can be useful in treating constipation and intestinal obstructions. They caution that it should be used with care as it can cause vibrations to be raised
or lowered, and therefore stir or smooth the emotions. It is a variable stone and individualistic
in its use. The color of the stone imparts an effect. Black can cause constipation, green a churn-
ing effect, yellow a smoothing flowing effect, and
blue an effect on the higher centers (e.g., lydic
center). They mention that tourmaline should not
be worn directly on the body.

Other properties ascribed to tourmaline include strengthening of the teeth and bones, contrac-
tion of varicose veins, and prevention of baldness.

Tourmaline is a gemstone of the Sixth Ray.

Turquoise

Composition: $CuAl_6(PO_4)_4(OH)_8 \cdot 4H_2O$

Crystallography: Triclinic

Form: Crystals are rare; it usually occurs in dense masses or concretionary aggregates.

Hardness: 5 - 6

Density: 2.84

Cleavage and Fracture: One perfect cleavage. Fracture usually even; sometimes conchoidal.

Color: Dark to pale blue, bluish-green, green.

Occurrence: Turquoise is a sedimentary mineral formed from the action of percolating ground water on aluminous rocks where copper is present.

Healing Properties: Paul Solomon suggests that it has a balancing and grounding influence and has recommended wearing the stone set in silver. Johnson's recommendations include wearing the gemstone in a ring on the left hand, wearing it as a pendant (with either teardrop or oval shape) worn over the heart, worn between the heart and throat, or held in the left hand while in a quiet mood. She felt that, when worn between the heart and throat, it would symbolize "the combination of love with will" for greater balance between them in order to be of service to others. Lama Sing considers it a very effective all-around healing stone which helps eliminate drosses which occlude or block functions of the ducts or bursa, and increases somewhat

lacteal flow and eliminates some carbon dioxide
from muscle tissue by stimulating the appropriate
vibronic forces.

Richardson/Huett believe that these stones
take on the characteristics of the wearer, and as
one is able to identify with his/her turquoise, he/
she will develop the ability to pick up the higher
qualities. The mineral carries great wisdom which
can help impart wisdom and understanding to those
of high sensitivity. It should be set in silver to
enhance its qualities. In healing, turquoise is a
personal stone and may be used for general healing.
They recommend wearing it in a large silver brace-
let on the left wrist.

Turquoise has been a very important gemstone
for the American Indian tribes of the West and the
Southwest. It was considered a holy mineral and
was a guardian of the tomb. It was also a very effective healing stone. The American turquoise is
often impure, and may contain small amounts of other
metals such as silver, gold, and iron. The impurity
content may influence its therapeutic properties.
This native mineral could be the most important of
the healing gemstones for Americans of all colors,
for all Americans have an Indian spirit, and the
Indian spirit is in the land.

In the East it was used for protection and
was considered a lucky stone and also a symbol of
prosperity. It was thought to have almost magical
powers capable of influencing both mental and physical forces, and is used even today for amulets.

Turquoise has been used to help heal a number of conditions. The blue-green color is healing
of itself and may be a major factor in its primarily being used to treat eye problems such as poor
sight and inflammations. This was done by placing
a stone directly on the affected eye to concentrate
the energies in that area. Turquoise has been used
to treat ailments of an inflammatory or feverish
origin; its color is soothing, and this may have
influenced the choice.

It is one of the gemstones reputed to change color in the presence of poison or other dangerous elements to its owner, and was thought to draw to itself the evil which threatens this person.

Turquoise is a gemstone of the Second Ray.

Zircon

Composition: $ZrSiO_4$

Crystallography: Tetragonal

Form: Crystals are often prismatic and/or pyramidal.

Hardness: 7.5

Density: 3.9 - 4.7

Cleavage and Fracture: Poor cleavage. Brittle.

Dispersion: High

Color: Reddish brown, yellow, grey, green, red, colorless. Colors can be induced by heating the mineral.

Occurrence: Zircon is found in igneous rocks and in pegmatites. It usually contains V, Th or Hg, which ultimately causes decomposition of the mineral.

Healing Properties: Zircon is a gemstone of the First Ray. Its keynote may be described as independence or self-dependence.

Richardson/Huett state that zircon tends to bring a more peaceful state to the wearer, and is useful in healing the spirit. It is best used by those of a quiet nature. It is also useful physically for treating some disorders of the lungs, predominently those of polio or tuberculosis.

This mineral may give off very low levels

of radiation which could affect the wearer.

The zircon was called jacinth or hyacinth until this century. It was recommended as an amulet to protect travellers against plague, wounds and injuries. It was also once believed to protect from lightning, and to help induce sleep.

Zoisite

Composition: $Ca_2Al_3Si_3O_{12}(OH)$

Crystallography: Orthorhombic

Form: Columnar, also radiate, granular or massive aggregates.

Hardness: 6

Density: 3.25 - 3.36

Cleavage and Fracture: One perfect cleavage. Brittle.

Color: Grey, greenish, brownish, pink, yellowish, blue to violet (Tanzanite).

Occurrence: Zoisite is found in metamorphic rocks, in metasomatized rocks and in hydrothermal veins. Zoisite is a member of the epidote group of minerals. A fairly recently discovered species, tanzanite, is the most notable gemstone of this group.

Healing Properties: A member of the epidote group, thulite, has been given as a gemstone of the Sixth Ray. Thulite is a form of zoisite, pink in color.

Tanzanite has the property of pleochroism, going from deep blue to purple to green depending upon crystallographic orientation. No healing properties have as yet been attributed to it.

5. Manner Of Functioning

The question arises regarding the manner in which these gemstones work to produce their effects. Certainly the colors of these minerals must be part of the overall healing vibrations. Color has been used not only in healing, but in creating "atmospheres" for many centuries, and the psychological and physical effects of color have been discussed in numerous books and articles.

In her book, Healing and Regeneration Through Color, Corinne Heline explains the philosophy linking the properties of gems, stones and metals with color and astrology. There are twelve zodiacal hierarchies which work with the mineral kingdom and "infuse into its component parts something of the force and rhythm which belong to themselves. All minerals and gems are therefore attuned to some one of the twelve constellations and proclaim this affinity by their color." When one wears or even possesses metals or jewels, he or she attracts the related planetary forces to him/herself. "The ancients held that every gem was originally crystallized by and around an entity which had a real though subjective (or inner plane) activity and awareness. This entity was capable of impressing the subconscious mind of the person possessing the gem as to coming events, thereby enabling him to avoid danger or to embrace opportunities. Hence the great importance of wearing jewels in harmony with one's stellar rays." Talismans were fashioned and worn, as they act as magnets, having a strong attraction for good or evil according to their use. She gives the following correlation between gems, metals, and color with astrological signs:

Table 4

Sign	Jewels	Metal	Color
Aries	Ruby, Bloodstone, Red Jasper	Iron	Red
Taurus	Golden Topaz, Coral, Emerald	Copper	Yellow
Gemini	Crystal, Aqua-marine, Carbuncle	Mercury	Violet
Cancer	Emerald, Moonstone	Silver	Green
Leo	Ruby, Amber, Sardonyx	Gold	Orange
Virgo	Pink Jasper, Turquoise, Zircon	Mercury	Violet
Libra	Opal, Diamond	Copper	Yellow
Scorpio	Agate, Garnet, Topaz	Iron	Red
Sagittarius	Amethyst	Tin	Purple
Capricorn	Beryl, Jet, Black & White Onyx	Lead	Blue
Aquarius	Blue Sapphire	Lead	Indigo
Pisces	Diamond, Jade	Tin	Indigo

But color is not the only factor, and usually is of secondary importance, in the use of a gemstone in healing. There are other aspects which must be considered. Lama Sing has commented that one should choose primarily crystals and secondarily by color.

Gemstones and metals appear to have an electromagnetic force strong enough to influence the cells of the body when placed on the body. Plants also have this effect to a lesser extent.

In a number of readings, Edgar Cayce referred to vibratory forces in gemstones which assist in stepping up the sensitivity of the body to become aware of what it is seeking. The forces which emanate from certain gemstones and metals work with similar forces within the individual and have an enhancing effect. This enables the person to attune to the creative forces of the universe. Thus, healing, spiritual enlightenment, etc., can occur. Their ultimate function is to help us to find our Christ selves. In this connection, it is possible that one of the effects of these crystals is to help release unused energies and power within the person by acting on the individual cells (perhaps even on the atomic level), stimulating the intelligence of these cells and atoms to correct the condition.

Gemstones and metals can protect a person from the electrical and magnetic radiations which constantly circulate in our universe. Pure metals emit an astral light which counteracts the negative pull of the planets. Gemstones, if of sufficient size and quality, are even more effective.

It may be possible that certain elements in the mineral can be brought into the body (in trace amounts) by direct contact, and these may be elements which the body has in insufficient supply. According to Lama Sing, living in an area of certain mineral deposits will have an effect on the brain wave faculty of the residents, and it will

differ from the faculties of other areas lacking
these minerals. Certain minerals containing the
missing elements can be imported to be used to com-
pensate for deficiencies.

Another theory is that certain gemstones
and metals act as condensers of cosmic energy from
the sun and have the ability to focus this healing
force on the bodies of the people who are wearing
them. Each gem has its own frequency of vibration
and will select certain ones to transmit to the
wearer.

In the theory of the seven rays, gemstones
are said to be similar in a way to tuning forks
having vibrations corresponding to those of some of
the higher emotions. This is discussed in the chapter on the seven rays, and will not be repeated
here.

Birthstones may also be effective. The i-
dea behind birthstones is that planetary influences
(electric and magnetic) radiate into space and become focussed by their responding gemstones. The
belief is that persons wearing stones to which the
months of their birth are dedicated will be render-
ed subject to the planetary influences (both good
and bad) by which their months are regulated in
their courses. The concept of birthstones goes
back to the first century A.D., when Josephus (its
originator) believed that there was a connection
between the twelve stones of the high-priest's
breastplate, the twelve months of the year, and the
twelve zodiacal signs. The custom of wearing the
birthstones probably began during the 18th century,
however, as the therapeutic powers of gemstones
were much more important. The importance of birthstones probably had been exaggerated.

The following lists are of birthstones of
various peoples and historical times (Kunz, p.315):

Table 5

Birthstones

	Jews	Romans	Isidore, Bishop of Seville	Arabians
January	Garnet	Garnet	Hyacinth	Garnet
February	Amethyst	Amethyst	Amethyst	Amethyst
March	Jasper	Bloodstone	Jasper	Bloodstone
April	Sapphire	Sapphire	Sapphire	Sapphire
May	Chalcedony Carnelian Agate	Agate	Agate	Emerald
June	Emerald	Emerald	Emerald	Agate Chalcedony Pearl
July	Onyx	Onyx	Onyx	Carnelian
August	Carnelian	Carnelian	Carnelian	Sardonyx
September	Chrysolite	Chrysolite	Chrysolite	Chrysolite
October	Aquamarine	Aquamarine	Aquamarine	Aquamarine
November	Topaz	Topaz	Topaz	Topaz
December	Ruby	Ruby	Ruby	Ruby

Poles	Russians	Italians	15th to 20th Century
January			
Garnet	Garnet Hyacinth	Jacinth Garnet	Garnet
February			
Amethyst	Amethyst	Amethyst	Amethyst Hyacinth Pearl
March			
Bloodstone	Jasper	Jasper	Jasper Bloodstone
April			
Diamond	Sapphire	Sapphire	Diamond Sapphire
May			
Emerald	Emerald	Agate	Emerald Agate
June			
Agate Chalcedony	Agate Chalcedony	Emerald	Cat's Eye Turquoise Agate
July			
Ruby	Ruby Sardonyx	Onyx	Turquoise Onyx
August			
Sardonyx	Alexandrite	Carnelian	Sardonyx Carnelian Moonstone Topaz
September			
Sardonyx	Chrysolite	Chrysolite	Chrysolite
October			
Aquamarine	Beryl	Beryl	Beryl Opal
November			
Topaz	Topaz	Topaz	Topaz Pearl
December			
Turquoise	Turquoise Chrysoprase	Ruby	Ruby Bloodstone

A correlation between the breastplate of the High Priest, Aaron, and the foundation stones of The Book of The Revelation has been suggested by some writers. In the book of Exodus, chapter 28, instructions are given to Moses for the design and manufacture of a holy breastplate which was to be composed in part of four rows each of three precious stones set in gold (King James Version). Upon each stone was engraved the name of one of the twelve tribes of Israel. There is ambiguity and therefore uncertainty as to the actual identities of the stones due to problems in translations and the correlation of ancient names of minerals with modern ones. There are, consequently, a number of lists published giving the stones of the breastplate. In a recent book by Richardson/Huett, the stones of the silver breastplate - which were employed ornamentally for a manuscript copy of the Torah used in an ancient synagogue - are described, and these were arranged in three (rather than four) vertical rows.

In The Book of The Revelation, chapter 21, John describes the Holy City of the New Jerusalem including the twelve foundation stones of the wall, which also correspond to the original twelve apostles of Jesus Christ.

The following lists of stones (on page 107) were taken from several sources and represent some of the best information presently available.

The cyclical nature of all living matter also must be considered. A gemstone that would be beneficial during one period of time may not be so (and even may have a negative effect) at another. According to Lama Sing, the variance in gems is due to celestial movements. Certain qualities would be amplified within the self under one set of astrological influences, and using a gem might give too much of that quality while diminishing another to a point which is detrimental to the self. He further states that there are electro-magnetic

Table 6
Stones In Aaron's Breastplate

King James Bible	Correction to The Bible	Foundation Stones in The Revelation
Sardius	Carnelian	Jasper
Topaz	Chrysolite	Sapphire
Carbuncle	Emerald	Chalcedony
Emerald	Ruby	Emerald
Sapphire	Lapis Lazuli	Sardonyx
Diamond	Onyx	Sardius
Ligure	Sapphire	Chrysolite
Agate	Agate	Beryl
Amethyst	Amethyst	Topaz
Beryl	Topaz	Chrysoprase
Onyx	Beryl	Jacinth
Jasper	Jasper	Amethyst

Kunz	Richardson/Huett
Red Jasper	Sard
Light Green Serpentine	Agate
Green Feldspar (Microcline)	Chrysolite
Almandine Garnet	Garnet
Lapis Lazuli	Amethyst
Onyx	Jasper
Brown Agate	Onyx
Banded Agate	Beryl
Amethyst	Emerald
Yellow Jasper	Topaz
Malachite	Sapphire
Green Jasper or Jade	Diamond

cycles as well as astrologic ones, both based on
date, time and place of birth. Wearing the zodiacal symbol of one's birth may be beneficial as it
may heighten the awareness of one's purposes for
being in the earth plane at this time. This sign
can affect vibrational frequencies drawn from the
cosmos and intensify them on a subconscious level
in the individual.

Lama Sing, in discussing gemstones, states
that they have the ability to amplify the vibration
of thought and also to further amplify the length
between the spiritual and the mental. Certain crystals, when placed on the forehead, enhance the ability of an advanced soul to be at one with its eter-
nal source. Endocrine centers can be affected by
the greater clarity of the levels of vibration
brought about by intensifying or purifying segments.

Some gemstones may also have an effect of
"coupling" the wearer better to the environment,
especially if they come from the area of residence.

In another theory, it has been suggested
that a charge travels from the gemstone to a planet
and back to the gemstone, and this produces a vibratory rhythm, particularly with the birthstone. We
need to know how to balance vibrations in all parts
of the body, especially the glands, and gemstones
have properties to accomplish this purpose. It is
important to match the vibrations of the stone with
the person, keeping in mind that different parts of
the body may have different vibrations.

Several psychics have recommended against
more than one person using the same gemstone, as
the vibrations from each would be in it, which then
could negate its beneficial effects and even have a
deleterious effect. If a stone is to be used on
more than one person, it should be "cleansed" before being transferred to the next person. Two
ways of cleansing a stone might be to subject it to
a weak magnetic field such as passing a weak magnet
over it, and burying it in the earth for a twenty-

four hour period (e.g., from sundown to sundown).
Exposure to sunlight probably also would be useful.
A suitable blessing of the stone would also be ef-
fective.

There is a theory held by Rudolf Steiner
and others that healing comes through the etheric
body and that plants therefore are the most effective therapeutic agents. But there are other tools
used in bringing about healing. William Tiller has
postulated seven levels of unique substance which
obey different kinds of laws and operate in different kinds of space-time frames. Two are body levels (physical and etheric), one is transitional
(astral), three are mind (instinctive, intellectual
and spiritual), and the seventh is spirit. These
substances inter-penetrate each other and may even
interact (weakly) with each other. The mind can
bring them into interaction. He further postulates
that there is a ratchet effect, that action begin-
ning at the mind level will work its way down
through other levels to produce an effect on the
physical level (and vice-versa). Drugs, surgery,
radiation and the like probably work mainly (if not
only) on the physical level, plants on the etheric
ratcheting down to the physical. The healings of
Jesus must have come from the spirit level. Healing can be initiated at any of these seven levels
and pass up or down. On what level do gemstones
initiate their workings? It may not be on either
of the two body levels, but on one of the mind levels. The effects may then pass upwards and down-
wards, perhaps not only producing physical healing
but also connecting the various levels in some people. There is also the possibility that they work
on the body level in a manner suggested by Tiller.

The glands (at the physical level) and
chakras (at the etheric level) are probably com-
pound glands (chakra-endocrine pairs) which can be
represented as a tuned circuit through which a person may tap energy from the cosmos. These coupled

pairs act in a laser mode (i.e., they work synchro-
nously to manifest coherent energy and then radiation from these centers). "The manifestation of
psycho-energetic phenomena is associated with tak-
ing the primary energies in the body and making
them coherent." It may be possible that gemstones
also work on the body levels and can affect this
"lasering" action.

We must not omit the psychological factors
in this discussion. The expectation of an event
often affects its happening. The belief that a
particular gemstone will help in correcting a particular condition will probably help in the healing
even just from holding a positive attitude. The
trust of the wearer may also have an effect on the
stone, enhancing its particular power. There may
well be a blending of the physical and mystical.

There are a number of factors, both objec-
tive and subjective, which probably influence the
effectiveness of precious minerals.

According to many psychics, and others,
the size of the gemstone is important; small stones
apparently have little effect while those of two
carats or more are effective. The quality of the
gemstone also is of importance; the nearer to perfection, the greater the benefit.

Another very important factor is the degree
of match of the vibrations of the mineral with
those of the subject person. Unfortunately, we
have no way as yet of measuring this phenomenon.
We do not even know objectively whether a particular gem is a good choice for an individual and
have to go through the process of trial-and-error
to make these determinations. Someone skilled in
radionics (use of the pendulum) would have an ad-
vantage in this matter, and this may well be as
good a way as any to select a stone.

Gemstones usually are cut into various
shapes, and different shapes, even in the same
species, may produce different effects or may pro-

duce the same effect at varying amounts of intensity. It may well be that each person is affected
individually by shape as well as species of gemstone.

Most natural minerals contain impurities to
a greater or lesser extent; the higher the quality,
the fewer impurities. They may be in the form of
physical inclusions (e.g., rutile in quartz) or as
substitutions of one or more chemical element(s) in
the crystal lattice. These impurities probably
have an effect, although it may well be small.
Once again, we do not know what to measure nor probably how to do it if we did. Impurities may enhance the properties of a gemstone. The American
Indians, for example, preferred turquoise with matrix rather than pure.

The mode of formation of the mineral also
must be considered, as well as its subsequent history. There are three groups of the formation of
rocks: igneous, sedimentary, and metamorphic.
Some rock formations have been reworked by nature,
perhaps a number of times, and many of the trans-
formations have been profound. Within each petro-
logic group are many different types of rock which
often grade into each other. How much has mode of
origin affected the vibrational properties of minerals? Is it possible that crystals of the same
species have different properties if they have different geologic origins?

Let us go even further into our enquiries.
There are currents within the earth and through the
upper part of the crust; they are probably not consistent with time. Most minerals are formed over a
long period of time, rather than quickly. It is
possible that this long time-span could have had a
damping effect on the earth currents as they may
have neutralized each other over a long period of
time. It may also be that these currents at the
time of exposure (the latest in the history of the
mineral) have some effect.

The position of the magnetic north pole
(which shifts frequently in small amounts, and oc-
casionally in large degrees) might well have an influence, particularly on those minerals which contain iron. Also, minerals from different geographic locations will have different angular inclina-
tions towards the pole.

Our planet is one of a number in our solar
system, and our system is a part of a galaxy. According to astrology, the positions of planets and
other heavenly bodies affect living matter, and
this has been and still is a subject of study by
many people. We know that the moon exerts a force
on the earth (at least its surface) and possibly
on its inhabitants. It is not unreasonable to suggest that extra-terrestrial bodies have an effect
on rocks and minerals, and can influence some of
their vibrations.

There are also atmospheric conditions to be
considered. If a mineral was formed at or near the
surface of the earth, it was affected to some extent by the atmospheric conditions at that time.
In many cases, the minerals would not have formed
without particular conditions. Even if the minerals were initially created at depth, they eventu-
ally became subject to external conditions (or we
should not have found them) through uplift, ero-
sion, etc. It is possible that the surface environment (including climate) has also affected vibrations. One can speculate that exposure to abundant
sunshine could even enhance certain vibrations.

These materials are crystalline and therefore have regular structures. One can question
whether crystallographic symmetry exerts an influence on therapeutic properties. We know that it
affects physical properties such as piezo-electricity.

The time of the day may play a role in
using particular stones. We know that the earth's
electromagnetic field differs during the 24-hour

day, and that this field has an effect on matter.
It is possible that gemstones differ in their res-
ponsiveness to this field at different times of the
day.

In ancient times, there were priests or the
like who were well-versed in the use of gemstones
for healing and other purposes. With their demise,
the information was essentially lost, and if we
wish to use precious stones today for therapeutic
purposes we have to rely on the judgment of the person selecting the mineral (who may be oneself or another). There is a great deal of guesswork involved, and erroneous choices can easily be made. It
is also time-consuming to try different stones, one
following another.
A further factor, and probably an important
one today, is that modern man (particularly in the
developed countries) has in good part become removed
from nature. We do not respond in a "fluid" manner
to natural phenomena as we are no longer attuned to
nature, having insulated ourselves (and our vibrations) from its vibrations. We may even have altered our vibrations by this removal from natural
living. Many are even out of harmony with nature.
Our lives have become increasingly complex; we are
more "sophisticated" and have become less open and
receptive, not only to the vibrations of nature,
but each other as well. There is a lack of faith
such as that which Jesus meant when he told people
to become as children. We have gotten away from
natural healing as well in our pursuit of a more
mechanical life-style. We have been violating nature in so many ways instead of working with nature.
We need to get back to more natural living. I do
not suggest that we return to primitive living and
discard everything in our civilization, for much of
what we have and know today is good and useful.
Natural living implies living with, rather than a-
gainst, nature, and we can do so in ways which are
suitable for our times and development. I suspect

that just eating a diet of real food would increase receptivity to earth vibrations.

We no longer have people trained in the use of gemstones in healing, and there is not good agreement in the literature about the properties of individual stones. The question may be asked: "How can we obtain more useful and reliable information with tools that are now available?" Use of the pendulum by one gifted in the art has already been suggested. Another way, which would take some time, might be to try something similar to homeopathic "provings", where a number of "normal" people would wear and/or ingest stones (or their powder) and their reactions would be recorded and studied to determine correlations. We know that different homeopathic remedies work on different types of people; a similar situation probably exists for gemstones.

We might also study the electric field around people to see if changes in this field can be detected when various gemstones are used. A person when healthy would have a different field than when ill. These fields are weak, and shielding would be necessary. There may also be a magnetic effect, but once again shielding would be necessary, and having a separate room would also be required, as the earth's electric field would otherwise cause too much interference. Equipment presently exists to perform these types of experiments.

Perhaps we could work with tissue cultures rather than people, although this would assume that the effect of gemstones is not a conscious one. Yet the tissues may contain elements of the consciousness of the organism from which they were obtained.

We might also employ psychics and study the effects on them as well as record their observations. Psychics may act as iron-core conductors, thus enabling measurements to be made.

There are approximately three thousand minerals found in nature; only a small number are regarded as gemstones, and not all of these are thought to have healing properties. A number of questions come to mind regarding this phenomenon, the first two being: Why are these particular minerals effective; and, Why are they gemstones (or precious metals)? Other questions include: Why are some gems more effective than others; Why are particular ones effective for certain problems; and, Why are so many minerals (the overwhelming majority) not effective?

In an attempt to find at least partial answers to these questions, I examined some properties of the gemstones described in this book to see if there were similarities which could be correlated. The first area investigated was crystallography, mainly basic building blocks and whether they were centrosymmetric or non-centrosymmetric. Some of these are given in Table 5 (page 116). We can see that, while most of the species are centrosymmetric, the presence or absence of a center of symmetry appears to have little if any effect on healing properties. An opal is amorphous, having only short range order. The types of building blocks and their spatial arrangement also do not display any pattern. What spectral information was available in the scientific literature failed to show any correlations. Geologic origin also gives no consistent information.

While composition and color probably play roles in effectiveness, there are many minerals with compositions and colors similar to these particular gemstones which do not have any known healing properties. One wonders then why it is that gemstones are healing stones. Perhaps it is not that way, but that in ancient times certain minerals were found to have therapeutic properties and these were highly valued, and called precious stones, and were later used decoratively.

Table 7

Mineral	Crystal Class	Building Blocks	Mineral Class
Azurite	2/m	Independent SO_4 tetrahedra	Sulphate
Beryl	6/mmm	Single rings of SiO_4 tetrahedra	Silicate
Chrysoberyl	mmm	Independent BeO_4 tetrahedra	Oxide
Chrysocolla		Sheet structure $(Si_4O_{10}$ tetrahedra$)$	Silicate
Copper	m3m	Cubic densest packing	Element
Coral (calcite)	$\overline{3}$m	Planar CO_3 groups	Carbonate
Corundum	$\overline{3}$m	Hexagonal close packing	Oxide
Diamond	m3m	Tetrahedral	Element
Feldspar (adularia)	2/m	Tectosilicate	Silicate
Garnet	m3m	Independent SiO_4 tetrahedra	Silicate
Gold	m3m	Cubic densest packing	Element
Hematite	$\overline{3}$m	Hexagonal close packing	Oxide
Jadeite	2/m	Single Si_2O_6 chain	Silicate
Lazurite	$\overline{4}$3m*	Tectosilicate	Silicate
Magnetite	m3m	Cubic close packing	Oxide
Malachite	2/m	Independent SO_4 tetrahedra	Sulphate
Nephrite	2/m	Double Si_4O_{11} chain	Silicate
Olivine	mmm	Independent SiO_4 tetrahedra	Silicate
Pearl	mmm	Planar CO_3 groups	Carbonate

Mineral	Crystal Class	Building Blocks	Mineral Class
Quartz	32*	Tectosilicate	Silicate
Silver	m3m	Cubic densest packing	Element
Spinel	m3m	Cubic close packing	Oxide
Topaz	mm2	Independent SiO_4 tetrahedra	Silicate
Tourmaline	3m*	Independent SiO_4 tetrahedra	Silicate
Turquoise	$\bar{1}$*	PO_4 tetrahedra	Phosphate
Zircon	4/mmm	Independent SiO_4 tetrahedra	Silicate
Zoisite	mmm	Independent SiO_4 tetrahedra	Silicate

---

* Non-Centrosymmetric

According to the philosophy of the Seven Rays, gemstones represent the highest development of the mineral kingdom and therefore have more power. They also are thought to contain permanent atoms (see the chapter on the Seven Rays). Perhaps minerals also go through many incarnations and have souls, or the equivalent. And just as some human entities are more advanced than others in their spiritual development in this incarnation, so it may be that some minerals have reached a higher stage of development, having passed through lower stages.

6. Use Of Crystals In Atlantis

It is thought by some investigators that the origins of the use of gemstones in healing were in the Far East, probably India, and go back to as early as 2000 BC. This writer believes that this practice is much earlier than that, dating back into pre-history in Atlantis. Psychic readings tell us that crystals were used by the Atlanteans for energy and also for healing. These readings appear to refer to synthetic crystals, which may have become dominant in the later stages of Atlantean civilization. But it is probable that the study and use of natural crystals for these purposes preceded synthetic ones.

Three psychics whose readings have been recorded have somewhat different impressions of some of the details as to their content, shape and manner of functioning.

Edgar Cayce mentioned an energy stone which he called the "Firestone" which was located in the middle of an oval building. This structure was lined with non-conducting materials (stone or metal) and had a retractable dome which could be rolled back to allow the rays of the sun to be received directly by the stone, and also energies from the stars. Energies from these sources were concentrated by passing them through prisms (or glass) to act upon instruments that controlled the various modes of travel. Vehicles used for transportation were not directly driven, but rather were remotely controlled from power stations. The force impelled from the stone acted upon the motivating force in the crafts themselves. (This implies that the

crafts had some kind of "intelligence" manufactured
into them.) The rays from the stone were a form of
"fire" and also were used for healing by regeneration, and would rejuvenate subjects to effect great
longevity. The stone (which was sometimes called a
Tuaoi Stone) apparently consisted of two sections,
a larger lower and a smaller upper section. It has
been described as a large cylindrical glass of hexagonal shape, faceted in such a manner that the capstone was designed for centralizing the power or
force that was concentrated between the end of the
cylinder and the capstone itself. There was no mention of the actual composition of either the cylinder or the capstone, and they may well have been of
two different materials. Nor was there mention of
whether they were intimately attached, perhaps even
grown one on top of the other, or just lightly
touching. In this stone, "light appeared as a means
of communication between infinity and the finite,
or the means whereby there were communications with
those forms from the outside". (Reading #2072-10,
Edgar Cayce). In later times it was developed into
the center from which energies radiated to power
and guide the various modes of travel. There were
a number of generations of these stones, and they
differed from each other. Rays from within the
earth itself as well as from the sun and stars were
focussed by the facets of these stones. He also
mentioned that there were crystals located in
"pits", and that the energies radiating from the
sun upon these crystals were converted through them
to the internal influences (energies) of the earth.
He mentioned gases used in connection with the
Tuaoi Stone for conveniences such as light, electricity, motion, etc.

In these readings, there is no mention made
of the compositions or structures of these stones.
They were called by several terms: glass, prism,
stone. One can speculate that perhaps some actual-
ly were clear, glassy materials similar to present-

day optical glass which were cut into special forms
to produce the desired effects. In current termin-
ology, fine glass is sometimes (commercially) called crystal. Also, some solid state lasers use
glass rods which have been doped with a rare-earth
element called neodymium. It seems more probable,
however, that they were crystalline materials mod-
elled after natural minerals which had previously
displayed special energetic properties. In one
reading, Cayce mentioned that precious stones were
used in Poseida (a portion of Atlantis), but he did
not say how or for what purposes.

Lama Sing, in discussing solar energy storage, indicated that the best method would be to use
a crystalline structure which would act to constantly recycle energy and amplify it. The facets and
cleavage would produce these effects in a manner
similar to that of Atlantis. Crystals can amplify
solar energy and the Atlanteans used their knowledge of crystal refraction, collection, amplification and storage to produce energy. A beam of
light directed intensely and focussed specifically
on certain series of facets on a gem will, when reflected, be amplified. The spectrum of energies
would be broken up into component wavelengths to be
more usable. The Atlanteans used the spectrum of
this energy for specific purposes. Certain ones
were used in agriculture, others for healing, knowledge or "increasement of substance". Some were
used for "disassembling molecular structures", for
construction, for molecular combination, transmu-
tation of matter, etc. "Crystals have the ability
to transfer energy, to retain it and maintain its
intensity, to focus and transmit it over great distances to similar receivers as are equal or compar-
able to the transmitter." The Atlanteans were thus
able to transmit energy from one pyramid to another.
The pyramids were part of a celestial and solar energy amplification system. The different levels
within them corresponded to the strata of the

energy. These strata had their effects at various points in the pyramid, and the pyramid acted as a focussing device.

He has stated that the source of power was based upon morphology (external crystal faces) and cleavage (both of which are reflections of the internal atomic arrangement) and the carrying agent. The crystals were supported in what he has called carrying agents. They were aligned with certain celestial bodies to produce a constant and endless source of energy. These crystal generators were not lasers nor laser-like in their manner of operation, but rather were the reverse of our present solid-state lasers.

The crystals were located in pyramids. These pyramids were constructed in a specific manner to single out the planet earth, and also to project the use of the crystals for energy purposes such as climate control, water flow, health, food storage, etc. There are forms of energy which relate to mathematical (geometric) patterns. The pyramid (an inverted cone) tends to have the effect of isolating vibrational frequencies. It acts as an amplifier enabling one to "hear" vibrations from great distances which can be transmitted and amplified for a variety of energy uses. The crystals were used to transmit and isolate certain frequencies which were to be used for these energies. The effect upon the physical body was to harmoniously balance the existing vibrations. The body consists of a varying number of specific frequencies which when combined are singular to that entity and its body. When it is diseased, there is discord within the body and the energies are in imbalance. The crystals were used to bring the vibrations into balance to regain health. Two crystals were used, one as a transmitter and the other as a receiver. Crystals were also used for energy storage, and these were surrounded by inert gases or were encased within certain types of alloys. The energy was similar to electrical energy but was much more advanced. In the peak (or capstone) of the pyramid was a miniature crystal shaped like a pyramid; it was very powerful, and a tuning device.

Aaron Abrahamsen has described the energy crystals in more detail than either Edgar Cayce or Lama Sing. He has indicated that these "energy forms" were concentrated within pyramids (the pyramid shape seems to have been important in their use), and many of these crystals had the shape of triangles, squares, ovals and circles. They were both two and three dimensional, depending upon function. Some may be discs, others hemispheres, pyramids, etc. The crystals were often coated with silica; mercury also was used as a coating. There was an opening at one end of the coating which permitted the life-giving beam to emerge from energy cells.

These crystals were used to provide power; each would seek its own level in order to produce the proper amount of power. When not in use, they were energized by large reflectors which gathered energies from the stars. This had the effect of re-orienting the crystalline structure, which regenerated them for further use. Crystals also were used in medicine in healing of the physical body (including surgery) and the mind; they had the effect of connecting the brain directly to God.

A number of methods were used to produce these crystals. In their development, they were very responsive to music, light and color. The nuclei and even the orbits within the crystalline structures were alive and responded strongly to music. Shape also was very important. A number of shapes were used including circular, square and triangular. They were faceted in specific forms and numbers. The odd numbers of facets (3,5,7) were used for particular diseases, while the even numbers were used to give energy to people already on their way to recovery. Colors also were used to give energy.

The formation of these crystals was a delicate operation. They were grown mostly from aqueous solutions. Simple crystalline structures of natural minerals were synthesized from a solution of salt, water, and other substances, which was allowed to grow in particular stems (directions). They were suspended within the solution and "the crystalline structure would adhere to the solution or the solution would form itself onto the basic matter. They had what they called a basic structure to start with". (Reading #1091 - A. Abrahamsen). The other substances in the solutions included acids from plants, and then bromide. At one time, iodide also was put in. After the solution was prepared, a very high frequency sound was produced to agitate the water, and to form a very fine film on top. The solution was then heated, while the sound was stirring it. The frequency of the sound controlled the crystal form, and by setting it to a specific frequency a specific form was made. After the sound had been turned off, music was played in the area and the crystals grew under the music. The music was performed on violins, harps, flutes and clarinets. Many of these structures were made to be healing stones.

The place where the crystals were synthesized was called the Laboratory of Life. It was a very serious (but not dour) place where joking and light conversation were not allowed. The people went about in an attitude of prayer because these crystalline structures could hear and be affected by the spoken word and became what they heard. There had to be complete cooperation of these people who were of the same mind and experiences, and who came together with the same purpose. The vibration level was very high in this laboratory, as each person spent a part of every day raising the vibrations. The attitude, while serious, was not sad. The music that was played for the crystals

was also heard by the people working there, and
they were beneficially affected by it. The people
worked together, cooperating with nature to find
the principles for growth to be used for the benefit of all.

Physicians prescribed energy crystals to
treat individuals for various ailments and also to
raise the vibrations of the bodies themselves.
Crystals were therefore made specifically for individuals following the prescriptions. Color played
an important role, too. Many of the crystals were
green, aqua and some were red. Lavender colored
crystals were used to treat cancer. These crystals
were rectangular and the structure was such that
the lines of the shape were parallel to the long
axis of the crystal itself. (This would suggest orthorhombic or tetragonal symmetry.) When the bone
was involved, the color of the crystal was aqua.
The crystals were shaped as either rectangles or
teardrops, the rectangle being more common. In
this form, the "crystalline structure" was diagonal
to the rectangular shape. The energy flowed in
this direction. White crystals of circular shape
were used for the eyes. They were placed over the
eyelids, and a band of four additional crystals were
in a belt which was placed above the eyelids at
night, even on the forehead, two above each eye.
Green crystals were used for the internal organs
(e.g., liver, kidneys, intestines, pancreas, etc.)
A rather large crystal was placed either on the ab-
domen, stomach or side, and held there overnight.
Sometimes they were worn during the day. The shape
of the crystal would be square, as was its crystalline structure. (Crystalline structure as termed
in these readings refers to the direction of the energy flow.) This crystalline structure would at
times have the appearance of a matrix, and the energy would emerge from each part of the matrix and
enter the internal organ(s) which required healing.
Red, particularly a deep ruby red, was used for the

joints of the hands and feet, and other joints as well. The crystal shape was circular.

Bella Karish has suggested that lasers or laser-like devices were used to grow at least some of the crystals. She also believes that atomic energy was involved in their use.

Edgar Cayce implied that crystals also were used in connection with energies within the planet. There are energies which travel through the earth in radiating patterns, meeting (and concentrating) in certain locations. It is reasonable to believe that the Atlanteans utilized these energies, and may well have gathered and transmitted them by means of suitable crystals. They also may have tied these energies into those from the celestial bodies; this has also been intimated by Cayce.

These readings are really quite vague, and at best only give a very small part of the whole picture. The description of the synthesis given by Abrahamsen gives little information and seems to this author to be too restrictive. It is difficult to imagine healthy humor being forbidden in the laboratory, as humor can be so healing. And the Lord certainly must have an excellent sense of humor, for there is so much of it about in this world. In none of the readings was information given regarding the compositions or structures of energy crystals, of the instruments used to control the flow of energy for transportation, construction, etc., nor of how the crystals transmitted energy to these devices. Both Edgar Cayce and Lama Sing have indicated that this knowledge will be obtained only by those who are pure in purpose and of high spiritual development. Lama Sing has further stated that we are not yet ready to receive this information. In our present overall level of consciousness, it is probable that it would be misused and disaster would result. After all, it was the misuse of the Tuaoi Stone which brought about the destruction of Atlantis.

The question may well be posed whether we
shall be able to use the information directly once
we are ready and able to receive it. Rudolf Steiner has discussed the development of "man" throughout time, and speaks of the differences between
present-day people and Atlanteans, and also of the
atmospheric and planetary changes which have occurred. According to Steiner, our bodies today are
denser than were those of the Atlanteans; our water
also is denser while our atmosphere is less dense.
Our animals and plants are different as is the physical appearance of portions of our planet. We are
less attuned to nature and have no control over the
"Life Force". We are, however, more developed in
thought processes (concepts and logic).

In the new age that is coming, we shall become better attuned to nature and our "psychic power" will be greater. Nevertheless, there will still
be differences between ourselves and the Atlanteans,
and in some ways they may increase. It seems un-
likely, therefore, that an exact transfer of tech-
nology would be reasonable. Modifications based u-
pon the current conditions and scientific knowledge
will probably have to be made. But we shall be
able to use the information from Atlantis as a base
for further development.

7. Future Use Of Crystals

It is reasonable to assume that crystals will be used in the future for energy purposes, and in fact are being used today in some applications. Solid-state (and gas) lasers are being utilized in photo-medicine and photo-biology for a number of purposes, including repair of detached retinas, irradiation and destruction of malignant tumors into which special dyes have been injected, photo-coagulation of gastro-intestinal bleeding, and treatment of glaucoma. Crystals of other materials are used for photo-voltaic purposes, and for acoustic and optical devices.

The scarcity of large, high-quality natural crystals coupled with their very high prices would preclude their use in general applications. Also, we can "tailor" synthetic crystals by the precise addition of impurities to obtain specific desired effects. We must expect therefore that the crystals that will be used for energy purposes in the future will be synthetic rather than natural.

We can anticipate that, in the near future, crystals will be increasingly used in electronic devices for both diagnosis and treatment. There will be a growing sophistication and use of such instruments as we learn more about vibrations in illness and health. They will be able to tune into the frequencies of the person to determine the presence and location of any aberrations, and also will be able to aid in retuning the body by supplying the necessary vibrations so that it can become balanced again. They may well also work on the mind level.

Further into the future, crystals will probably be used essentially by themselves to detect out-of-place vibrations and to make necessary corrections. These will in all likelihood also work on higher levels of the person to help in tuning the mind and spirit areas, and thus aid the person to become whole.

There are possible dangers as well as advantages involved in the use of synthetic crystals, dangers which directly relate to their production. In preparing to make a crystal for a specific purpose, one or more impurities would be added to the mix (substituting in small part for other cations normally present in that species) to produce the spectrum of energy desired. We are thus able to obtain only the energy frequencies (which appear to be) necessary for a particular healing (or for other purposes). This higher level of purity could also have drawbacks, which may be serious. In the natural mineral, there probably would be a number of impurities present which would have their energies represented, although on a much lower level of intensity. Also, the amplitude of the major peak of the desired impurity would be somewhat lessened. In the synthetic crystal, only the spectrum of the added impurity would be present and the major peak (which might be the only peak) would be intensified. A graphical illustration is given in Figure 2, page 130. The "energy" produced would be intensified and could therefore be too strong and also too pure. The additional impurities of the natural crystal may have a beneficial moderating effect - similar to that of plants where the use of just the "active" ingredient in a drug often produces adverse side effects, while the use of the entire leaf or root or even the plant itself does not, as the other ingredients act to affect or prevent these side effects.

Furthermore, synthetic minerals lack many of the vibrations of the earth which develop over

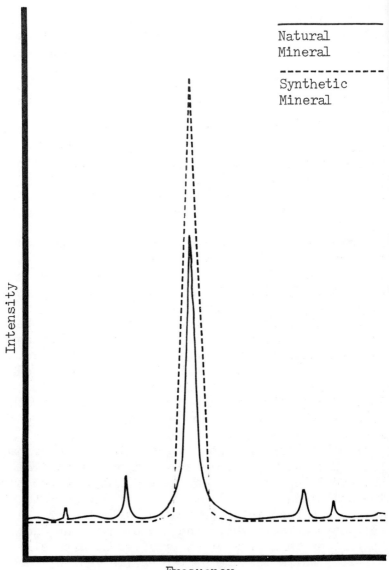

Natural
Mineral

Synthetic
Mineral

Hypothetical Spectra of
Energetic Frequencies of
Natural and Synthetic Minerals

long periods of time in natural minerals. The natural minerals have had a long time in or on the
crust of the earth to be affected by these vibrations and to develop a natural balance. Synthetic
crystals, on the other hand, are grown rapidly -
over periods of several hours to a few weeks. Also
they have the vibrations of the people growing them,
of the people and locale of the chemical plants
that synthesized their components, of the building
where they are grown and the equipment used to grow
them, the gas or liquid atmosphere in which they
were grown, etc., as well as natural effects from
the air, sun, ground, etc. There will be little in
their brief histories to mellow them. The large
and possibly moderating earth effects will be missing.

As an aside, I believe that it may well
have been that the breakup of Atlantis was due only
in part to the mistuning of the Tuaoi Stone. These
synthetic crystals had, amongst others, the vibrations of the people who grew them, and they were of
rather low quality amongst members of the Sons of
Belial. These were the people who became trapped
in materiality, and misused their creative powers
in self-indulgence. They selfishly exploited their
surroundings, including the life contained therein,
to such an extent that the true spiritual value of
man was lost to them. It is also possible that
they were too pure and therefore lacked natural moderating influences, and thus could be tuned too
highly. It may well have been that part of the
problem therefore was brought about by the synthesis of the crystals which allowed the mistuning to
be possible.

There are undoubtably ways to offset these
possible negative effects of synthetic crystals,
some of which will be mentioned here.

The synthesis of the starting materials and
the growth of the crystals should be performed under the most careful of conditions and by people

especially selected for this purpose. Only those
of high spiritual development would perform these
tasks. The building in which they are grown would
be located in energetically favorable geographic
areas. The atmosphere within these buildings would
be conducive to a high level of thought and beha-
vior. Abrahamsen has spoken of good music being
played in the buildings where the crystals were
grown in Atlantis. Beautiful music (and beauty in
general) is beneficial in many ways and certainly
would raise vibrations, whatever played. It would
help in mellowing and making crystals more beneficial, and in bringing in universal forces to act in
a grounding manner. The buildings would be aesthetically pleasing in architecture and in decor.

We may use these synthetic crystals in conjunction with natural objects such as plants and
flowers, and perhaps even with natural minerals to
get the earth effects which would balance and mellow those of the crystal. We may also be able to
find ways to get these stones to couple directly
into the currents within the earth and thereby obtain earth effects. Perhaps burying them in ground
which has well-developed beneficial vibrations
would meet this purpose, at least in part.

They could also be used in conjunction with
beauty, both natural and man-made. While being
treated, the person could be observing or producing
objects of fine art, listening to or performing
fine music, watching graceful dancing or even par-
ticipating in dance with good rhythm. They could
be used while the person was in a beautiful natural
setting. They could also be used with specific
healing colors and perhaps simultaneously with music or art.

The use of precious minerals in healing,
while an ancient form of therapy, is a new concept
in medicine today. We still have much to learn a-
bout this subject, but we probably have sufficient
information to use at least some of the stones now,

if only experimentally. In the future, one would
expect that medical personnel will become increasingly involved in this type of therapy (as well as
others of an esoteric nature) to aid patients in
becoming whole. Precious stones are another tool
to be added to the armamentarium of the healer.
They probably work predominantly on the mental level, but also to a lesser extent on the spiritual
and physical levels. As consciousness is raised,
people will become increasingly receptive to this
and to other forms of esoteric treatment. We must
never forget, however, that all healing is from
God, as we are of God. And that which we call
death can also be a healing, and here gemstones can
be used to help a person make the transition smooth-
ly from this plane to the next.

Appendix One

Chemical Elements

Symbol	Name	Atomic Number	Atomic Weight
Ac	Actinium	89	227
Ag	Silver	47	107.8
Al	Aluminum	13	26.9
Am	Americium	95	243
Ar	Argon	18	39.95
As	Arsenic	33	74.9
At	Astatine	85	210
Au	Gold	79	196.9
B	Boron	5	10.8
Ba	Barium	56	137.3
Be	Beryllium	4	9.01
Bi	Bismuth	83	208.9
Bk	Berkelium	97	247
Br	Bromine	35	79.9
C	Carbon	6	12.01
Ca	Calcium	20	40.08
Cd	Cadmium	48	112.4
Ce	Cerium	58	140.1
Cf	Californium	98	249
Cl	Chlorine	17	35.4
Cm	Curium	96	247
Co	Cobalt	27	58.9
Cr	Chromium	24	51.9
Cs	Cesium	55	132.9
Cu	Copper	29	63.5
Dy	Dysprosium	66	162.5
Es	Einsteinium	99	254
Er	Erbium	68	167.2

Symbol	Name	Atomic Number	Atomic Weight
Eu	Europium	63	151.9
F	Fluorine	9	18.9
Fe	Iron	26	55.8
Fm	Fermium	100	257
Fr	Francium	87	223
Ga	Gallium	31	69.7
Gd	Gadolinium	64	157.2
Ge	Germanium	32	72.5
H	Hydrogen	1	1.008
He	Helium	2	4.003
Hf	Hafnium	72	178.4
Hg	Mercury	80	200.5
Ho	Holmium	67	164.9
I	Iodine	53	126.9
In	Indium	49	114.8
Ir	Iridium	77	192.2
K	Potassium	19	39.1
Kr	Krypton	36	83.8
Ku	Kurchatovium	104	257
La	Lanthanum	57	138.9
Li	Lithium	3	6.94
Lr	Lawrencium	103	256
Lu	Lutetium	71	174.9
Md	Mendelevium	101	258
Mg	Magnesium	12	24.3
Mn	Manganese	25	54.9
Mo	Molybdenum	42	95.9
N	Nitrogen	7	14.007
Na	Sodium	11	22.9
Nb	Niobium	41	92.9
Nd	Neodymium	60	144.2
Ne	Neon	10	20.1
Ni	Nickel	28	58.7
No	Nobelium	102	255
Np	Neptunium	93	237
O	Oxygen	8	15.9
Os	Osmium	76	190.2
P	Phosphorus	15	30.9

symbol	Name	Atomic Number	Atomic Weight
Pa	Protactinium	91	231
Pb	Lead	82	207.2
Pd	Palladium	46	106.4
Pm	Promethium	61	147
Po	Polonium	84	210
Pr	Praseodymium	59	140.9
Pt	Platinum	78	195.1
Pu	Plutonium	94	242
Ra	Radium	88	226
Rb	Rubidium	37	85.4
Re	Rhenium	75	186.2
Rh	Rhodium	45	102.9
Rn	Radon	86	222
Ru	Ruthenium	44	101.1
S	Sulphur	16	32.06
Sb	Antimony	51	121.7
Sc	Scandium	21	44.9
Se	Selenium	34	78.9
Si	Silicon	14	28.1
Sm	Samarium	62	150.3
Sn	Tin	50	118.7
Sr	Strontium	38	87.6
Ta	Tantalum	73	180.9
Tb	Terbium	65	158.9
Tc	Technetium	43	99
Te	Tellurium	52	127.6
Th	Thorium	90	232.03
Ti	Titanium	22	47.9
Tl	Thallium	81	204.3
Tm	Thulium	69	158.9
U	Uranium	92	238.03
V	Vanadium	23	50.9
W	Tungsten	74	183.8
Xe	Xenon	54	131.3
Y	Yttrium	39	88.9
Yb	Ytterbium	70	173.4
Zn	Zinc	30	65.3
Zr	Zirconium	40	91.22

Appendix Two

Glossary of Terms

Acicular: In slender, needle-like crystals.

Botryoidal: In groupings of globular forms (also tuberose).

Cleavage: The breaking of a crystal along regular surfaces which are related to the crystal structure. Cleavage is always parallel to a possible crystal face. The quality of cleavage varies from perfect (where the surface is smooth and lustrous, and the crystal is difficult to break along any other direction) through good (where the mineral breaks easily along the cleavage, but also can be broken along other directions) to imperfect (where the ease of fracture along the cleavage plane is only slightly more pronounced than along other directions.

Columnar: In stout, columnlike individual crystals.

Dendritic (also arborescent): In slender divergent branches, somewhat plantlike, composed of distinct crystals.

Density: See page 29.

Dispersion: The separation of visible light into its color components by refraction or diffraction. It is seen as the play of colors in a mineral, particularly one that has been cut and polished. It is directly related to the index of refraction. The higher the index, the greater the dispersion (in transparent crystals).

Dodecahedral: Describes a twelve-sided figure, with diamond-shaped faces.

Ferro-magnesian: Having a relatively high content of oxides or iron and/or magnesium.

Fibrous: In slender fibre-like aggregates.

Filiform: In thread-like crystals.

Fracture: The breaking of a non-cleavage surface. There are several types, the main ones being conchoidal (like that of glass, curving and shell-like) and hackly (jagged, irregular surface).

Hardness: See page 29.

Index of Refraction: An optical property which is related to the velocity of light as it passes through a substance. It can be viewed as the ratio of the velocity of light in air to that in the solid.

Lamellar (also tabular): The mineral consists of flat plate-like members super-imposed and adhering to each other.

Lustre: A visual impression produced by the reflection of light from the surface of a mineral. Its intensity is dependent upon the index of refraction, not the color of the mineral. It is divided into two types, metallic and non-metallic. The latter is sub-divided into vitreous (appearance of broken glass), adamantine (brilliance of lustre, as the diamond), resinous, silky and pearly.

Massive: Irregular form without distinct characteristics.

Octahedral: Describes an eight-sided figure, with equilateral triangular faces.

Parting: Resembles cleavage, but differs in that it is not always present in all specimens of the mineral.

Pinacoidal: Forms which have two faces which are parallel to two axes.

Prismatic: Describes a figure with rectangular faces.

Pyramidal: Describes a form whose faces intersect all crystallographic axes.

Rhombohedral: Describes a six-sided figure with each face a rhombus (equilateral parallelogram).

Tetrahedral: Describes a four-sided figure with isosceles triangular faces.

140

Bibliography

Abrahamsen, Aaron. Readings. AIM, P.O. Box 5008,
    Everett WA 98206.

Anonymous. "Gems, Stones and Metals for Healing
    And Attunement." Heritage Publications,
    Virginia Beach VA 23458. 1977.

Arem, Joel E. The Color Encyclopedia of Gemstones.
    Van Nostrand Reinhold Co., New York. 1977.

Bord, Janet and Colin. The Secret Country. Walker
    & Co., New York. 1977.

Carley, Ken. "Lapis Lazuli." The ARE Journal, 10,
    161-169. 1975.

Cayce, Edgar. Readings. Gems and Stones. ARE
    Press, P.O. Box 595, Virginia Beach VA
    23451. 1967.

Clark, Linda. The Ancient Art of Color Therapy.
    Pocket Books, New York. 1978.

Fernie, William T. The Occult and Curative Powers
    Of Precious Stones. Rudolf Steiner Publi-
    cations, Blauvelt, New York. 1973.

Gilluly, J., A.C. Waters, and A.O. Woodford. Prin-
    ciples of Geology. W.H. Freeman & Co.,
    San Francisco CA. 1959.

Health Research Compilation. Color Healing. Health
    Research, CA. 1956.

Heline, Corinne. Healing and Regeneration Through
    Color. DeVorss & Co., Marina del Ray CA.
    1975.

Hodges, Doris M. <u>Healing Stones</u>. Pyramid IA. 1961.

Karish, Bella. Personal communication. 1978.

Kostov, Ivan. <u>Minerology</u>. (transl. by P.G. Embrey & J. Phemister). Oliver & Boyd, London. 1968.

Kunz, George F. <u>The Curious Lore of Precious Stones</u>. Dover Publications, New York NY. orig. 1913.

Putnam, William C. <u>Geology</u>. Oxford University Press, New York, NY. 1971.

Richardson, Wally and Lenora Huett. <u>Spiritual Value of Gemstones</u>. DeVorss & Co., Marina del Ray, CA. 1980.

Rogers, Frances and Alice Beard. <u>5000 Years of Gems and Jewelry</u>. F.A. Stokes, New York NY. 1940.

Sing, Lama. <u>Benefits and Detriments of Talismans, Stones, Gems and Minerals</u>. ETA Foundation. 1977.

Sing, Lama. <u>Solar Energy</u>. ETA Foundation. 1977.

Sing, Lama. <u>Atlantis</u>. ETA Foundation. 1975.

Sing, Lama. <u>The Pyramids.</u> ETA Foundation. 1975.

Solomon, Paul. Readings. Fellowship of the Inner Light, P.O. Box 206, Virginia Beach VA 23451.

Spock, L.E. <u>Guide to The Study of Rocks</u>. Harper & Row, New York NY. 1962.

Steiner, Rudolf. <u>Cosmic Memory</u>. Rudolf Steiner Publications, West Nyack NY. 1959.

Stewart, C. Nelson. <u>Gemstones of The Seven Rays</u>. The Theosophical Publishing House, Adyar Madras, India. 1939.

Tiller, William A. "Energy Fields and The Human
    Body, II." ARE Medical Symposium, 5, 70.
    1972.

Tiller, William A. "Three Relationships of Man."
    ARE Medical Symposium, 8, 75. 1975.

Tompkins, Peter & Christopher Bird. The Secret
    Life of Plants. Harper & Row, New York NY.
    1973.

Mineral Index